Desire and Dissent

NEW DIRECTIONS IN EUROPEAN WRITING

....

Editor: John Flower, Professor of French, University of Exeter.

ISSN: 1350-9217

As the twentieth century draws to a close we are witnessing profound and significant changes across the new Europe. The past is being reassessed; the millennium is awaited with interest. Some, pessimistically, have predicted the death of literature; others see important developments within national literature and in movements cutting across frontiers. This enterprising series focuses on these developments through the study either of individual writers or of groups or movements. There are no definitive statements. By definition they are introductory and set out to assess and explore the full spectrum of modern European writing on the threshold of a new age.

Previously published titles in the Series:

Allyson Fiddler
Rewriting Reality: An Introduction to Elfriede Jelinek

C. Davies
Contemporary Feminist Fiction in Spain: The Work of Montserrat Roig and Rosa Montero

NEW DIRECTIONS IN EUROPEAN WRITING

Desire and Dissent

An Introduction to Luis Antonio de Villena

Chris Perriam

BERG
Oxford / Washington, D.C.

First published in 1995 by
Berg Publishers Limited
Editorial offices:
150 Cowley Road, Oxford, OX4 1JJ, UK
13590 Park Center Road, Herndon, VA 22071, USA

© Chris Perriam 1995

Library of Congress Cataloging-in-Publication Data

A catalogue record for this book is available from the Library of
Congress.

British Library Cataloguing-in-Publication Data

A catalogue record for this book is available from the British Library.

T

ISBN 1 85973 057 4   *1 0 0 3 3 3 4 5 9 X*

Printed in the United Kingdom by WBC Book Manufacturers,
Mid-Glamorgan.

Contents

Acknowledgements

Some of the material in Chapter Two was presented in a paper at the XIII Congreso del Mediterráneo in Murcia 1990 and my special thanks are due to José María Álvarez and the regional Consejería de Cultura for their parts in organising this conference and a subsequent Fiesta de la Poesía in Murcia. The paper appeared in a reworked version in the *Monographic Review* and I am grateful for permission from the editors to reuse some of this material; parts of discussion of poems from *La muerte únicamente* have appeared in the *Bulletin of Hispanic Studies,* and again I am grateful to the editors for permission to reuse some of this material. Chapters Three and Six contain material previously presented in a paper given at the Second Conference on 'Questions of Homosexuality' (June 1992) organised by the Institute for Romance Studies of the University of London and I would like to record my gratitude to the members of the organising committees of both conferences.

I am also very grateful to Luis Antonio de Villena for opening up so many new directions through his writing, for making valuable suggestions about – and indeed corrections to – a late draft of the book, and for being patient, courteous, helpful and brave about what he feels is the 'strangeness of being turned into an object for study'.

The Publications Board of the University of Durham made a generous grant to help with the financial costs of publication of this book.

I am indebted to the following for permission to reproduce extracts from Villena's works:

Luis Antonio de Villena for *La tentación de Ícaro* © 1986.
Luis Antonio de Villena and Laertes S.A. de Ediciones for *Para los dioses turcos* © 1980 and *Amor Pasión* © 1986.
Luis Antonio de Villena and Mondadori España S.A. for *Chicos* © 1989.
Luis Antonio de Villena and Visor Libros for Villena, *Poesía (1970–1984)* © 1988 and *Como a lugar extraño* © 1990.
Luis Antonio de Villena and Editorial Planeta S.A. for *Fuera del mundo* © 1992.

Preface

In line with the general aim of the series, this book is deliberately not a definitive 'scholarly' statement but rather a set of suggestions and new directions. Since I have not been writing primarily for those with a specialist interest in literatures in Spanish and since I certainly have been writing with some rather Anglo-Saxon attitudes, there are some aspects of Villena's work (as he himself observed after seeing a late draft) which have been only briefly indicated and some, necessarily, which have been omitted altogether. Also, I have used the bare minimum of reference to academic studies and reviews directly about Villena or other Spanish writings and I have restricted myself to only a handful of contextual and theoretical points of reference, where possible written in English, taking for granted a certain degree of familiarity with what I hope we can still call non-establishment critical discourses (particularly feminist and gay).

Since I am always telling my students not simply to recount what 'story' a text tells, I have felt I too should have the grace to avoid doing this: so this introduction is not made up of plot summaries and paraphrases. My approach has been to quote and translate fairly extensively from a reduced selection of texts and to try to place them contextually in various ways. In the body of the text short quotations from prose works are given in my own English translations but with page references to the Spanish text; occasionally, where a phrase in Spanish is of special interest or is ambiguous, the original Spanish is given in parentheses. More substantial quotations are given in the Spanish first, with a rough, working version in English immediately afterwards. Villena's use of Spanish is often unorthodox, especially in the matter of neologism and punctuation, and for the purposes of this introduction to his work I have at times erred on the side of inappropriate sobriety.

Introduction

uis Antonio de Villena, today one of the best known and most colourful figures on the cultural scene in Spain, is a self-consciously unconventional subject. His poetry and prose, as well as his appearances in public, on television, at state- or regionally-sponsored cultural events, or out at night, are all concerned with formulating an Art of Living. As a consequence and as a prerequisite of this, his writing has strong personality. Being also an Art of Love, however, it is at the same time concerned with uncertainties, and with incoherence. Engaging with the erotic causes the writing or the loving subject to lack stability, and the object of desire to be unknowable. Further complexity is given to this unknowability and instability by the fact that, for Villena, the erotic is defined in terms of the transgressive and in particular the homoerotic. Villena is also writing an Art of Dissidence and therefore involved with what is proscribed, unreliable and open to question in the various cultures which, although they seem to have created the strong personality of his texts, or his self, also challenge their integrity.

The narrators and voices of the texts persuade their readers into reconstructing for themselves an authorial personality who appears to be firmly rooted in established cultures. They have, however, a tendency to shift into discourses of dissent which go counter to such a grounding or into markedly artificial writing which overuses and exhausts the cultural references which might otherwise have made the personality cohere, if that is what as readers we wanted. In many of Villena's poems, but particularly in his prose writings, there are compelling, seductive voices who establish themselves in the reading imagination as figures whose perspectives on life make them reliably like sources very close to the author. Similarly, it is now generally considered in Spanish literary circles that Villena, consistently for some and obsessively for others, is constructing a life's work, an old-fashioned *oeuvre* made out of experience and art, that revolves around the relations of beauty, desire, nostalgia, and love.[1] However, these texts and their voices are always challenging us not to believe in these lives and voices in any straightforward way, and not to in a way which is vital to our attraction to them. On the one hand his texts construct a now unmistakable voice for contemporary Spanish readers, as unmistakable as his deep, grave, frivolous, erudite, humorous and affected voice on television, and conference or festival stage; on the other hand his written texts and the lived experience they represent valiantly deny the validity of the concept of an essential, coherent self. Villena's writing is excessive and evasive and yet engages in a clear dialogue with established cultural and literary conventions as much as with dissident, counter-cultural preoccupations. While it represents a strong, centred, special individual it also gaily deconstructs the very notion of such a figure.

When in 1990 the prestigious literary magazine *Litoral* dedicated a special issue to him it was clear that he might as easily be aligned with the big names in twentieth-century Spanish poetry and thought, who from *Litoral*'s inception in 1926 have peopled its pages, as with those who have been represented more readily in its issues on Erotic Poetry, Rock Poetry, Prison Poetry or the gay Catalan poet Jaime Gil de Biedma.[2] Most of the contributors to the Villena volume feel attracted to the radical undecidability of his personality as much as to the revolutionary importance and the seriousness of his writing. On the first page of text the guest editor makes immediate reference to Villena as a personality both praised and reviled in equally powerful measure, to 'the actual Villena, and Villena the legend' (*Pujante deseo*, p.7). 'We know,' the text continues in the light of this,

1. The most recent crystallisation and critique of this view is Leopoldo Alas, 'Notas para una lectura *heterodoxa* de la obra poética de Luis Antonio de Villena', *Cuadernos hispanoamericanos*, no. 475 (1990), pp.146–8. (Leopoldo Alas, who was born in 1962, is not to be confused with the nineteenth-century novelist of the same name.) See also Francisco Javier García Rodríguez, 'De la belleza al deseo: del deseo a la muerte. Aproximación a la obra poética de Luis Antonio de Villena, 1971–1984', *Tropelías* (Zaragoza), 2 (1991), pp.41–7.
2. *Luis Antonio de Villena: Sobre un pujante deseo*, Special Issue of *Litoral* (Málaga), 19° Año Literario, no. 188 (1990), edited by Jesús García Sánchez. *Litoral* was founded in 1926, in Málaga, and in its various phases has published and discussed influentially such figures as Vicente Aleixandre, Luis Cernuda, Manuela de Falla, Joan Miró, Pablo Picasso and María Zambrano. The special issues I refer to here are numbers 61–3, 151–6, 185 and 163–5 of the most recent series (that of the 'Años literarios').

that his first public appearance was as a singer of period variety songs and that his original vocation was that of a television chat-show host. Perhaps because of the mania he has for smothering his fingers in rings, what he does has passed relatively unnoticed: scandalous scenes after dark, dubious company, ejection from cinemas for shameful behaviour, etc. (pp.7–8)

For Leopoldo Alas Mínguez in his portrait of Villena in the same volume (pp.13–21) 'what was said about him and what he himself revealed to us was no more than a collection of metaphors, interpretations, narrative possibilities' (p.13). For Javier Marías, in an 'Imaginary Portrait of the Artist At Home' (pp.73–5), quite simply and symbolically 'Villena is never to be seen at home' (p.73). All this evasiveness makes the brief biographical entrée – that most traditional task of the writer of an introductory study – entertainingly difficult to approach.

Although Alas, who refers to his subject throughout as His Perversity, suggests that 'Rumour ran about the city that [...] His Perversity had been born at Antioch three centuries before the birth of Christ' or 'in Alexandria beneath the silken wing of the Ptolemies' (p.13), Luis Antonio de Villena was born in Madrid in 1951 and grew up (as so many of his almost-autobiographical stories indicate) surrounded by an extended family of elegant, strong, and sharp-minded women. In his early teens he travelled frequently to Paris, becoming fluent in French and imaginatively allied to French cultural and literary traditions. He studied Classics and Modern Languages at the Universidad Complutense at Madrid from 1968 to 1973, a period whose intellectual and political turbulence both provided the raw experience and sparked the stylistic rebelliousness which characterise his first published writings. An exotic rarity in difficult political times, Villena's first collection of poems, *Sublime Solarium* came out in 1971, full of 'a strange surrealism [...] and militantly luxurious vocabulary'.[3] *El viaje a Bizancio* (*The Journey to Byzantium*) appeared five years later, covering the period 1972–4, with titles like 'The Beautiful and the Damned', 'Reseña de estatuaria griega' ('Reviewing Greek Statuary'), 'Dominio de la noche' ('The Dominion of the Night') and 'Monumento en honor de Lord Byron' ('A Monument in Honour of Lord Byron'). In 1979 and 1981 *Hymnica* and *Huir del invierno* (*To*

3. Luis García Montero, 'La poesía de Luis Antonio de Villena', in *Pujante deseo*, pp.53–8 (p.54).

Flee from Winter) marked a transition from a poetry focused on beauty, the exotic, the decadent and the playfully multicultural towards more painful concentration on the contradictions of desire and, in the poems written between 1981 and 1984 and collected in *La muerte únicamente* (*Death Alone*: 1984), on death. *Como a lugar extraño* (*As To A Foreign Place*: 1990) brings Villena closer at times to his solemn and erudite predecessor Luis Cernuda (1902–63) than to his earlier self, but also picks up on earlier streetwise tones and urban themes and anticipates *Marginados* (*Outcasts*) of 1993, a series of poems on some of the human casualties of late capitalist society.[4]

In parallel with the poems of the 1970s Villena had begun his long and now very distinguished career as literary critic, essayist and serious newspaper columnist, initiating a continuing dialogue between his prose writing and his poetry. Translations of Sandro Penna and Joachim du Bellay also enrich the context.[5] There are writings on youth culture, translations of texts by Balzac, Baudelaire and Barbey d'Aurevilly (with a prologue), a study of Oscar Wilde, and essays and reviews of a wide range of literature from the *Satyricon* though troubadour poetry, French decadent novelists and the poet and novelist Juan Gil-Albert, to (in an essay of considerable scholarly and critical importance) Cernuda.[6] In the 1980s and early 1990s the range of his literary criticism in short reviews and longer, more academic articles has extended hugely, attesting to a considerable dedication and seriousness.[7] In newspaper and magazine columns he has written on subjects as diverse as boys on motor-scooters, the New Right, Richard Gere and Cindy Crawford's affirmations of their sexual orthodoxy, and the attitude of the Catholic Church towards same-sex partnerships.[8]

4. Discussions of this collection and of the novel *Divino* (1994) have had to be omitted from this study which, apart from these opening pages, was completed in the summer of 1992. A select bibliography of Villena's work, with full references to the more substantial texts mentioned here, is to be found on pp.206–7.
5. *Quince poemas de Sandro Penna*, translated by Luis Antonio de Villena, Valencia, 1979; Joachim de Bellay, *Sonetos*, translated and annotated by Luis Antonio de Villena, Madrid, 1985.
6. Villena has been prolific in the writing of short studies, introductions and prefaces. Readers of Spanish wanting to follow up bibliographical leads might refer first to the 'Bibliographical Note' in Chris Perriam, 'Reality and the Angels: Luis Antonio de Villena and *La muerte únicamente*', *Bulletin of Hispanic Studies*, no. 67 (1990), pp.31–42, p.40.
7. Readers are referred to the Select Bibliography and to discussions of a number of these texts in the chapters to come.
8. *Cambio 16*, 1 August 1988, p.50; *El País*, 26 April 1989, p.13; *El Mundo*, 13 May 1994, p.2, and 24 June 1994, p.2.

Introduction

A key text of the 1980s is *La tentación de Ícaro* (*The Temptation of Icarus*, 1986), a set of linked essays which construct and reconstruct a personal ethics and aesthetics and which, in the view of at least one critic, tell us more about Villena (rather than the legend) than does the apparently autobiographical *Ante el espejo: Memorias de una adolescencia* (*In Front of the Mirror: Memoirs of an Adolescence*, 1981).[9] At the time of writing, Villena's career as a writer of non-fiction has culminated in two full-length biographical studies of Michelangelo and Leonardo da Vinci published in 1991 and 1993 (the former of these mingling fictionalised autobiography with biography and scholarly appraisal), a collection of essays on sexuality and desire – *El libro de las perversiones* (*The Book of Perversions*, 1992) – and an important study on Spanish poetry in the 1990s in an introduction to the anthology *Fin de siglo* (*Fin-de-siècle*, 1993).

Known at first for his poetry, Villena is now also firmly established as a novelist. *Fuera del mundo* (*Beyond the World*, 1992) and *Divino* (*Divine*, 1994) are both published by the mainstream firm Planeta and have had considerable impact, as has *Chicos* (*Boys*, 1989). This sequence of interlinked short stories in part builds on the subject matter and style of earlier short fictions in *Para los dioses turcos* (*For the Turkish Gods*, 1980) and *En el invierno romano* (*In the Roman Winter*, 1986). These texts, at once defiantly old-fashioned and emphatically modern, present to the reader dissident heroines and heroes (among them implied narrators) and transgressive desires, some of which – like the love of quite young men – are likely to sorely challenge even those for whom the word transgressive comes easily. Like his poetry, the early narrative works are unfashionable and often extremely highbrow in their choice of times, places and styles and mix the sparsely neo-realist with the richly poetic or the sheer outrageous. In them a nostalgic gaze moves in a glorious and dynamic sweep through cultures gay, popular, decadent, conventional and marginal. In *Amor Pasión* (*Amour Passion*, 1983, revised and augmented 1986) and *Boys* the narrators, by living and loving to the full, construct a counter-cultural version of the Madrid of the 1970s and 1980s, the years of transition and change in Spain from the late days of the dictatorship to the González governments.

In particular Villena has been writing, in these prose narratives,

9. Rafael Conte, 'Luis Antonio de Villena: Narrador del fin de siglo', in *Pujante deseo*, pp.39–42 (p.39).

against the grain of a number of influential trends in Spanish narrative of the time: the novel of middle-class marital break-up and nervous breakdown in comfortable surroundings, so popular in the yuppie years, is countered by a sustained critique of heterosexual consumerism and manners; the long-established novel of nostalgia which yearns for youth and the safety of the family in a pre-political world is countered by a vision of youth as a site of anything except innocence; the panoramic chronicle of the life and history of a great city, another money-spinning mode, is eschewed for a fastidious and highly selective account of some very unrepresentative lives; and the experimental novel, with its arresting difficulties, obliquities and discontinuities, stands in stark contrast to the ample, linear, pleasure-laden manner of Villena. For much of the time he is concerned with modern, urban desires and perspectives formed in the matrix of the cultures of homosexuality. His city is emphatically modern Madrid and Villena and his narrator-protagonists frequent a recognisable set of streets, bars, galleries, restaurants and discos; but the city is treated opulently and its locations are elevated, as in the feature films of Almodóvar, to theatrical status, lovingly piled high with the most extravagant symbolism and distracting detail.[10] It is often as if Madrid were the centre of some legendary decadent empire built out of fragments from other eras and geographies. Echoes and images of al-Andalus, of seventeenth-century Spain, renaissance Florence, Europe at the *fin-de-siècle*, Morocco or the Mediterranean (as the archive of classicism, route to the aesthetic Mecca of Italy, and as a bridge to the Orient and Africa) are all apt to intervene, enrich and disrupt the tales of the city. These narratives offer snatches of brilliant lives, artifice, fragments of desire, hard-nosed observation, chronicles of post-modern times and extravagant historical fiction; they shift from participating in the discourses of up-market gay writing to denying the validity of such a category of writing from positions which are, variously, libertarian, utopian and deliberately distant from the sexual politics of the 1970s and 1980s.

Towards the end of *In Front of the Mirror: Memoirs of An Adolescence* the narrator looks at why he puts himself into the very conventional framework of the image of the mirror:

10. See Paul Julian Smith, *Laws of Desire: Questions of Homosexuality in Spanish Writing and Film 1960–1990*, Oxford, 1992, Chapter 5, 'Pedro Almodóvar's Cinema of Desire', pp.163–203, and 'Coda: ¡*Atame!* . . .', pp.204–15; also pp.51–2 on the transgressive effects of 'excessive' detail in the writings of Terenci Moix.

Siempre me han gustado los espejos. De niño me miraba de continuo y aún lo sigo haciendo, y lo que veo en la pulida luna no es al *enemigo* ni el raro sortilegio que atemoriza a Borges, sino que me veo mejor a mí mismo, con más libertad y claridad, y así en él, me entiendo. Me he maquillado delante de los espejos, he disertado conferencias, he jugado a cambiar de personalidades, he cantado y he soñado mis propios gestos de amor, mi propia desesperación amorosa . . . [...] Todos escribimos, como dice Valéry Larbaud, con una máscara en el rostro, *un masque à l'ancienne mode de Venise*, pero esa máscara somos nosotros en medida igual que lo que haya detrás de la máscara, y que acaso sólo valientemente nos atrevemos a llamar rostro. Somos el rostro, la deformación, la máscara, la pintura, lo que nos cuentan, lo que nos suponemos, lo que soñamos, lo que creemos, y también lo que realmente, al decir cotidiano, somos. (*Ante el espejo*, p.187)

I have always liked mirrors. As a child I used to look at myself continually, and I still do; and what I see in the polished glass is not *the enemy* or the extraordinary apparition which so frightens Borges, but myself, seen in a better, more free and clearer light, and so by looking I understand myself. I have put on make-up in front of mirrors, pronounced lectures, played at changing personalities, I have sung, and dreamed up my own loving gestures, my own despair in love . . . [...] We all write, as Valéry Larbaud says, with our faces covered by a mask, 'a mask in the old Venetian style', but we are this mask as much as we are whatever there may be behind the mask and which perhaps only through bravery do we dare to call our face. We are the face and the distortion, the mask, the depiction, we are what we are told, what we suppose, what we imagine, what we believe, and what, in the everyday sense of it, we really are.

We need to read this passage as we need to read much of Villena's writing, for its curious angles. Though we might take the idea of the reflection head-on as an archetype of autobiographical writing, and accept easily the claim of improved focus on the subject, we are also expected to follow refractions out and away from anything so common and unfashionable as a stable, unified, delimited, individual sense of self. At one angle is projected the public-speaker and the serious reader (of the well-known Borges and the more obscure Larbaud, a characteristic combination);[11] at another angle is the intimacy of low-key theatricality. At one angle again,

11. Mirrors are ubiquitous in Borges, but the text Villena probably has in mind is 'Los espejos velados' ('The Draped Mirrors') in *El hacedor* (translated by Mildred Boyer and Harold Moreland as *Dream Tigers*, Austin, 1964). The line from Valéry Larbaud is to be found in 'Le masque', in Larbaud, *Oeuvres*, Paris, 1958, p.47.

imagination, inspirations, the representations of love, a straight and an old-fashioned Romantic sensibility; at another, a robust and up-to-date awareness of the social construction of reality, the relativity of beliefs, and the constant fragmentation of self and subject through and in language and representations. An awareness above all of the polish on the glass, not, therefore, even of its own surface let alone its depth. A feel for elegant slippages and evasions. An introduction, that is, to Villena's knowing scepticism about the myths of a salvational and unifying individuality which are affirmed or constructed in some of our favourite narratives of desire. Also, though, there is a hint of his fond indulgence of these myths.

The various evasions and the maskings in these texts, while clearly disallowing any naive and reactionary reading of them for an authorial origin, a unitary and unifying source, the Man behind the Work, do not conversely and conveniently add up to a denial or an absence of a strong conforming presence, to the 'death of the author'. Neither his ethics nor his aesthetics would make any sense if Villena were not allowed this problematic illusion of authority, this rather old-fashioned operation of the suspension of disbelief which allows us as readers also to pretend, to perform, and to desire in front of the mirror: to come to see again that 'we are [...] the mask, the depiction, we are what we are told [...] and what [...] we really are'. It is an illusion of authority which relies on marginality and the questions surrounding it, on a sustained shift in the relations of one subject position with another, on one look in the polished glass intersecting another.

Of the characters depicted in *For The Turkish Gods* Villena says 'they are, like myself, illustrious and marginalised. Socially displaced, hopeless obsessives on a quest for an impossible realm' (*Dioses turcos*, p.187). Similarly, in his 'Prólogo en tono de confidencia' ('Prologue In A Confidential Tone') to the 1986 pamphlet *Marginados* (*Poems On the Margins*) Villena says '[the texts] are about people and situations which have been left in a corner, or marginalised, like me in fact' (*Marginados*, 1986, p.11).[12] Despite the supposedly 'confidential tone', this remark advertises what is now, in cosmopolitan Spain at least, a cultivated open

12. This pamphlet, or *plaquette* as Villena prefers to call it, was published at Valencia by the literary magazine *La Pluma del Águila*. The title *Marginados* is reused as the title of the more substantial collection (Madrid, 1993) briefly described above.

secret: Villena's literary career has been built on a highly conscious and obsessively eccentric identification with unfashionable, forgotten, forbidden and exotic cultural scenes and artistic personalities; and his non-literary experience is a sustained flirtation with marginality.

In Villena's texts, beauty is closely and lovingly studied, but, precisely because of this, its attainment is a question of artificial rehearsal and emulation. The contemplation of the mirror, in the text quoted above, shows that true love is located in the before and after, not in the present, in the rehearsal and anticipation or in the aftermath of despair, but not on this side of the glass. Pronouncements from Villena the well-known critic and commentator are also performance, this text suggests. Two conventionally valued artistic skills, imaginative projection into other characters and singing (which is bardic, operatic, lyrical, deep emotional utterance), are revealed as bathroom- or bedroom-mirror experiences as much as the supposed timeless gifts of communication which are (or used to be) said to close the gap between desire and its objects.

The fullest introduction to date of Villena's poetry, by José Olivio Jiménez, sees the early collections, up to *To Flee from Winter*, as 'the history [...] of Desire.'[13] Jiménez's emphasis on the uniqueness of the individual's experience perhaps favours the kind of focus on the unproblematic, whole self which Villena's writing both teasingly invites and makes hard to sustain, but it also emphasises (if coyly) the fact that in *To Flee from Winter* 'beauty comes to mean the proximity of a young and finely-formed body, in certain concrete circumstances [...] in which the poet plays a part' (p.20). Later Jiménez is able to move much nearer to factors which disrupt clear reflection of the writing subject: 'Villena's poetry is poetry of the body, and poetry sustained by an attitude of rebellion at the ethical core, at the nerve-centre' (p.52). While creating this 'ethical core', Villena has been writing his way through and also counter to a period of radical change in literary and sexual-political cultures in Spain. Although he is an extremely literary writer he evades as often as he uses the conventions and traditions of highbrow writing, and these evasions are centred upon that 'poetry of the body'. As well as rewriting the aesthetics and radical ethics of the

---

13. José Olivio Jiménez, 'La poesía de Luis Antonio de Villena', in Luis Antonio de Villena, *Poesía 1970–1984*, Madrid, 1988, pp.9–64, p.9.

decadents and dandies of the beginning of the century in a way which chimes with a contemporary cosmopolitan hedonism (such as represented in Almodóvar's *The Law of Desire*), he has his poetic voices, narrators and characters stand in conflictive relation to contemporary literary tastes. His texts champion and assimilate some literary voices now (as in the past) mostly out of favour on the Spanish literary scene, in particular writers such as Barbey d'Aurevilly, Baudelaire, Rubén Darío, Huysmans, Octave Mirbeau, Rimbaud and Wilde. Villena has, moreover, openly aligned himself with the traditions of sexual and political dissidence surrounding popular gay culture in present-day Spain and homosexual culture in Spanish literature. From these positions his writing and living become involved in a rebellious counter-cultural ethic.

Two recent full-length studies by Ángel Sahuquillo and Smith (*Laws*)[14] have suggested that readings of this culture and its instabilities represent a major new (if overdue) challenge to Hispanic Studies. Sahuquillo's study is concerned mainly with poetry and is the first full-length study to attempt to theorise and politicise readings of the major gay Spanish poets born before 1936; Smith's book, focusing on later prose-writers and film-makers, is a theoretically more sophisticated, similarly ground-breaking study which begins to redress the omission by Hispanic Studies of the findings, problems and discourses of Anglo-Saxon Lesbian and Gay Studies. By reworking in his creative and critical writing many of the classic themes, styles and strategies of this counter-tradition, rather than follow more publishable trends, Villena has engaged in a transgressive and assertive rewriting of Spanish cultural history. At the same time – the more to infuriate the conventional and the traditionalist reader, but also to perplex the politically

---

14. Ángel Sahuquillo, *Federico García Lorca y la cultura de la homosexualidad masculina*, Alicante, 1991; this is a revised version of his previously published doctoral thesis *Federico García Lorca y la cultura de la homosexualidad: Lorca, Dalí, Cernuda, Gil-Albert, Prados y la voz silenciada del amor homosexual*, Stockholm, 1986. Also in the Hispanic context, see David William Foster's *Gay and Lesbian Themes in Latin American Writing*, Austin, 1991 (predominantly about prose narratives), which, although it is a curiously unproblematised presentation of some 'works that treat gay concerns and experiences' (p.1), does offer translations of some passages of little-known texts; *Now the Volcano: An Anthology of Latin American Gay Literature*, San Francisco, 1979, edited by Winston Leyland is a better, but now less obtainable, point of reference for Latin American gay writing in translation. For accounts of the male homosexual tradition in poetry specifically see Robert K. Martin, *The Homosexual Tradition In American Poetry*, Austin, 1979, and Gregory Woods, *Articulate Flesh: Male Homoeroticism and Modern Poetry*, Yale, 1987.

Introduction

correct – he re-reads with an almost indecent adoration the iconic texts of High Culture. In common with Lorca, and two other prominent homosexual poets Cernuda and Francisco Brines (b.1932), Villena is hypersensitive to the odder corners of excess or austerity in late Romanticism, the Spanish 'Golden Age', the Italian Renaissance and the Arabic, Latin and Greek classics.

One of Villena's early masks, or faces, and a surviving one, is that of a dandy for this new *fin-de-siècle*: he is nostalgic for earlier rebelliousness but ready to cross over flagrantly into a here and now of the specifics of sex and sexual culture in the metropolis. 'Dandyism', as he says in the essay 'El dandy como rebelde' ('The Dandy as Rebel') in *Corsarios de guante amarillo* (*Corsairs in Yellow Gloves*, 1983), 'is basically atemporal [...] the dandy is metaphor, brilliance, luxury, the "affirmation", as Oscar Wilde said, "of the absolute modernity of Beauty".'[15] Many of the protagonists, speakers and narrators of Villena's texts come to us from this angle of rebellion, and whereas it is clear that Villena's principal published voice is firmly homosexual from early on (there are coded but strong enough suggestions in *Sublime Solarium*), most of his lovers, adventurers, dandies and masks function in a context of sexual non-conformity (which includes a refusal to entertain categories of homosexual, gay or 'queer').[16]

> To be a dandy [...] is to adopt an attitude of rebellion: of individualistic romanticism. The dandy is opposed to social roles, to sexual dichotomy (the dandy often crosses into the terrain of the so-called 'feminine'), opposed to uniformity, to collectivism, to rules and morality. [...] For

15. *Corsarios de guante amarillo*, Barcelona, 1983, pp.39 and 41. The quotation from Wilde is in 'A Few Maxims for the Instruction of the Over-Educated', *The Complete Works of Oscar Wilde*, London, 1990 (reprint of second edition, 1966), p.1, 204. The subject of Wilde's sentence is in fact 'dandyism' rather than 'the dandy'.
16. In the various languages of Spain 'gay' exists, with 'gai', and is used generally, as are the less properly understood 'lésbico', 'lésbica' and 'lesbiana'. 'Queer' (and 'lo queer') has only recently begun to make a signifying impact on the Spanish scene, although the equivalent 'maricón' has long since been reclaimed by flamboyant radical tendencies in the major cities. Representations of radical drag have a long and distinguished history: see for example Alberto Cardín's short stories 'Renata Saldaña' in *Detrás por delante*, Montanés del Vallés, 1978 and 'La guerrilla de Macías' ('Macías's Little War') in *Lo mejor es lo peor*, Barcelona, 1981, and Copi (pseudonym of Raúl Damante Taborda), *El baile de las locas*, trans. Alberto Cardín and Biel Mesquida, Barcelona, 1978 (also contains Cardín's 'Diccionario succinto para el lector no entendido'. Cardín is an important literary source for the usages of the reclaimed term 'maricón'. See also Leopoldo Alas Mínguez *La acera de enfrente* (Madrid, 1994) – a semi-jocular emploration of contemporary gay lifestyles and terminology.

the dandy, homoeroticism is not mere scandal, or just another aspect
of his rebelliousness (in the same way as is abandoning a fine lady
having seduced her, or savouring the pleasures of incest), rather it is
something more. For he rejoices, as I have said, in ambiguity [...]
Moreover, the dandy sees in 'Greek love' one of the forms of Satan to
honour, an aspect of Evil by which he lives his life and which society
condemns. It is another form of rebellion. (*Corsarios*, pp.19 and 24)[17]

In Oscar Wilde he sees that 'art and life [...] are comprehended
through the same code' (p.101) and he is acutely aware of just this
double coding in his own textualisation of experience and his
experience of texts. Like Wilde, as read by Jonathan Dollimore,
Villena engages, if indirectly, in 'a critique of those ideologies of
selfhood which seek redemption in and through the individual,
especially the idea of a deep authentic subjectivity [showing] how,
in being true to that self, his contemporaries [are] more often than
not simply being true to their social identification'.[18]

The dandy's aesthetic, which Villena is constantly reworking (if
no longer actually living out) is, he notes, 'metaphor, discourse' and
'mask' (*Corsarios*, p.41). Desire, writing, and the dynamics of sexual
orientation exchange the same comprehending code in this
discourse. Unsurprisingly, at this stage in the century and in his
social, literary and sexual context, Villena knows that to narrate
your 'own' experience, to acknowledge your body as the text, is to
generate a movement of dispersal (a loss of self into discourse, a
cascade of shifting positions) as much as it is to stimulate strongly
that sense of unique experience, that reference back into the feeling
self which comes with a good story, or good sex, a flash of
remembrance, an exciting poem or a falling into love. The position
is perverse and paradoxical and often Villena's is, as Dollimore puts
it, a 'trangressive aesthetic' whereby 'insincerity, inauthenticity and
unnaturalness become the liberating attributes of decentred
identity and desire' (*Sexual Dissidence*, p.14).[19] Like Wilde, though
with one hundred years' more dissident complexity behind him,
Villena reinstates 'that which society forbids [...] *through and within*
some of its most cherished and central cultural categories'

17. By extension of the principles explained in the Preface I have decided not
to reproduce the original Spanish text in most of the cases when I am quoting
critical or other forms of not strictly imaginative writing.
18. Jonathan Dollimore, *Sexual Dissidence. Augustine to Wilde, Freud to Foucault*,
Oxford, 1991, pp.7–8. Dollimore is discussing 'The Soul of Man Under Socialism'.
19. On the 'paradoxical perverse' see *Sexual Dissidence*, pp.14–17 and 103–30.

(Dollimore, *Sexual Dissidence*, p.15).

'Un arte de vida' ('An Art of Life'), written in 1976 (*Poesía*, p.168), makes the dissident point from another angle and again discovers that the transgressive and the conventional intersect:

> Vivir sin hacer nada. Cuidar lo que no importa,
> tu corbata de la tarde, la carta que le escribes
> a un amigo, la opinión sobre un lienzo, que dirás
> en la charla, pero que no tendrás el torpe gusto
> de pretender escrita. Beber, que es un placer efímero.
> Amar el sol y desear veranos, y el invierno
> lentísimo que invita a la nostalgia (¿de dónde
> esa nostalgia?). Salir todas las noches [...]
> Dejar de amanecida tan fantásticos lechos,
> y olerte las manos mientras buscas taxi, gozando
> en la memoria, porque hablan de vellos y delicias
> y escondidos lugares, y perfumes sin nombre,
> dulces como los cuerpos.

> Live doing nothing. Attend to the unimportant, / your tie for the evening, the letter you are writing / to a friend, an opinion on a painting, given / in a talk but which you would never have the poor taste to pretend / was written down. Drink, since it is an ephemeral pleasure. / Love the sunlight and wish for summer, and for slow, slow winter / which invites nostalgia (but from where / such nostalgia?). Go out each night [...] / [...] / Leave behind such wondrous beds at dawn, / and smell your hands while you search for a taxi, reliving / your pleasure in memory, for they speak of soft hair on flesh, delights / and secret places, and nameless perfumes, / as sweet as bodies.

At their most rebellious the texts return to considerations which seem to be encrusted in convention, pairings of pragmatism and idealism, reality and desire, ecstasy and death. However, the essay 'Del suicidio y la muerte' ('Of Suicide and Death') in *The Temptation of Icarus* links such pairings both to the ethics and aesthetics of the marginal, or the 'extreme' as the text has it:

> ¿Merece, pues, la pena vivir? Ya he dicho que merece – y conviene – intentarlo, aun siendo conscientes del casi inevitable fracaso, si nos resistimos a caer en el convencionalismo de confundir *felicidad* con *bienestar*. Y ello es lo que valora la figura del *perdedor* genuino. [...] Si el *perdedor* es un tipo o un género ilustre, ello se debe a su desprecio a la norma, y al salto que efectúa para intentar atrapar una quimera, un imposible. (Sea el *vuelo* o la propia intensidad de lo bello quienes le destruyan.) [...] *Intentar* vivir, y comprender (y gozar) el valor de ese

intento. Porque amar la felicidad y amar el placer son extremismos. 'Quien baila se consuma', dice un poema de Aleixandre. Vale por quien vuela, quien se atreve, quien osa, quien desprecia, quien no se conforma, quien lo intenta, quien no cede, quien sabe que caerá y ama la caída. (*Ícaro*, p.102)

Is it, then, worth one's while to live? I have already suggested that the effort is of worth – and advisable – even if we are conscious of almost inevitable failure; so long as we resist the downward pull toward the accepted convention of confusing *happiness* with *well-being*. And it is this which makes the figure of the genuine *loser* so valuable. [...] If the *loser* as a class or type is noble as such, it is precisely because of his disdain for the norm, the leap he will make to try and capture some fantastic dream, to have the impossible. (Whether it is the upward *flight* itself or the intensity of beauty which destroys him.) [...] Attempt to live, and understand (and savour) the value of this effort. For loving happiness and loving pleasure are forms of extremism. 'Those who dance are made complete', says a poem of Aleixandre's. The same is true of those who take flight, who venture, dare, disdain, do not conform, who make the attempt, do not surrender, who know that they will fall and love the falling.

The presence of the poet Vicente Aleixandre is a reminder of the cultural trajectories through which Villena likes to take his dissidence. Aleixandre symbolises the link, via surrealism, back to Byronic Romanticism, *fin-de-siècle* rebellion and that whole dissident network within and outside the dominant Spanish literary culture of the first half of the century which Villena teases and uses. But as a much translated and respected Nobel Prize-winning poet, Aleixandre is no straightforward rebel. Far from it. He is, rather, in his quiet way an ideally problematic dissident figure. Aleixandre's homosexuality was until the 1980s a very closely kept secret and is to all intents and purposes invisible at the surface of his well-known published work (much of which appears at first to be classic heterosexual mysoginistic surrealism).[20]

Aleixandre hovers silently – who knows if through admirable

20. Daniel Eisenberg's entry on 'Spain' in Wayne R. Dynes ed., *Encyclopaedia of Homosexuality*, New York, 1991, pp.1, 236–43, includes Aleixandre with Lorca, Cernuda, Emilio Prados, Manuel Altolaguirre and Pedro Salinas (the latter two as bisexual) and suggests that the marking of the tercentenary of the death of Góngora in 1927 by the poets of the so-called Generation of 1927 'was a celebration of poetry, of Andalusia [...] an exuberant revolt against Spain's cultural establishment, and also an affirmation of Spain's homosexual tradition' (pp.1, 240). Sahuquillo, in his Preface to *Cultura homosexual* (most of the work for which

refusal to conform to type or just plain reactionary discretion –
around 'the world of homophilia', to use Villena's arch and
productively evasive phrase.[21] However, he is read by Villena
elsewhere as being strongly aligned with the 'rebellious ethic' of
surrealism, and thus with 'true liberalism [...] which today [that is,
1976] we would call *counter-cultural*'.[22] Rebelliously Villena puts
aside conventional readings of the high figures of modern Spanish
literature in this essay. Aleixandre is joined by the French *poètes
maudits*, by Emilio Prados (one of the poets studied by Sahuquillo),
by Lorca seen as 'writing from a position of rebellion and personal
crisis' in *Poet In New York* and *The Public*, and by Cernuda, in
anguished celebration of 'pleasure [...] and, moreover, the body of
the forbidden adolescent male', 'in his high-minded unorthodoxy
[...] always a surrealist' ('Vicente Aleixandre', pp.34–6). Hence,
through such lines of intertwining associations, the language of 'On
Suicide and Death' and the whole counter-cultural discourse which
gives the poems and stories their perverse dynamic: the association
of conformity with a dull death-in-life; of pleasure with falling;
writing with ascent; orgasm with both these; death with intensity;
and, in an old, still powerful pun common to English 'die' and
Spanish 'morir', of death with orgasm. A set of associations which
is further enlivened by Villena's early insistence on the primacy of
'ecstasy in the text' ('éxtasis en el texto') in the prefatory 'Inicial'
of *The Journey to Byzantium* (*Poesía*, p.115).

Alas reads this multiple position and follows the shifts of the
subject through desire in a pithy and necessarily slightly ironic
literary character analysis 'as amateur psychologist [...] friend and
reader of this controversial poet, this exceptional patient' ('Notas',
p.146). He offers the following description of an evasive dynamic
in Villena's gazing on the text of his desire:

> the most beautiful bodies, rather than referring to ultimate beauty refer
> to themselves and to their inevitable decline. Each erotic experience
> is no more than a sign of a higher experience (that of spiritual union
> in beauty) and is therefore always disappointing, being always the sign

---

was done in the early 1980s), notes that his decision not to include the still
surviving Aleixandre in his study caused surprise, but adduces the poet's silence
on the subject: two other surviving figures, Dalí and Gil-Albert were, on the other
hand, quite willing to talk (p.9).
21. Used in a discussion of the character Leopoldo in *Chicos*, p.76.
22. 'Vicente Aleixandre, el surrealismo y *Pasión de la tierra*' in Vicente
Aleixandre, *Pasión de la tierra*, ed. Villena, Madrid, 1976, pp.11-92, p.28.

but never the idea itself [...] But as it happens, it suits our poet that every experience should in the end be disappointing in this way. For life is, for him, precisely this quest and evasion; never being content with what one has and less so with the frustration of not being able to attain what one desires. Only by seeking what cannot be found can Villena avoid finding himself in the presence of what he does not want: a reality which he detests because it is laden with banal routine, mediocre, incapable of entertaining risk and passion. Our patient wants at all costs to escape this reality; to do so, he cannot cease to seek something other, and so as not to cease the search he must always renounce what he comes upon.

Life, then, is the art of playing off realities against fantasies, sex objects against idealisms. Even the doubly tragic sense of loss when a love adventure goes wrong – and there is neither the dream nor the body to hold fast to – is itself a triumph and a fulfilment. Villena generates satisfaction from nostalgia and perversity alike, he finds plenitude and perfection in absence more than presence, and as a post-modern artist he ekes pleasure wryly out of knowing fragmentations, parodies, and reinscriptions of codes of taste and value.

The 'secret' pleasures and transgressions of the poem 'An Art of Life', and of so much of Villena's writing, while tracing a swift escape from any normative moral centre, are revealed as having an open debt to cultural conventions and to ordinary 'reality' (in which, after all, he glories). His writing places him, or represents him, as being both at the centre and on the edge of involvement in the production of the new cultural possibilities of Spain after Franco; his verses and narratives become lines of desire drawing away from, intersecting, and retracing both a specific socio-cultural history and a symbolic, counter-cultural but compromisingly Romantic representation of a special, different and outlawed self.

1

Culture, Counter-Culture

Sexual and Cultural Politics

S ome of Villena's prose narratives look back on the final years of Franco's dictatorship to construct what to many of us is an unfamiliar reading of the period. Villena does not offer the view which is in common circulation and which sees the whole period of the dictatorship as a unitary dark age of sexual and cultural politics awaiting the kiss of democracy and liberal monarchy, nor does he attempt an objectivist chronicle of the times; instead he prefers to engage with the spectre of oppression more equivocally.[1]

The emergent sexual, and specifically gay, politics of Western cosmopolitan cultures in the wake of 1968 does not bypass the Spanish nations, despite the historical circumstances of the early 1970s when the last years of the dictatorship – and of the dictator's life – produced an ideological tightening-up and moral panic.[2] Either side of the death of Franco – which in *Boys*, significantly, is often just another event in the middle of some erotic or dissident saga which it scarcely interrupts – alternative groupings became established in Barcelona, Madrid and the large regional cities, and the treatment of alternative sexual politics in the left-aligned press which emerged from 1974 onwards is suggestive of continuity of debate rather than a sudden change of awareness.[3] The publication of Villena's textually and sexually extremely unorthodox *Sublime solarium* in 1971 coincided with the emergence of a new gay culture

---

1. For a review of socially committed writing of the 1960s and 1970s in Spanish literature, see John Butt, *Writers and Politics in Modern Spain*, London, 1978, pp.53–65.

2. See Raymond Carr and Juan Pablo Fusi, *Spain: Dictatorship to Democracy*, London, 1979, Chapter 9.

3. The radical magazines of the period 1974–6 give ample evidence of this; among the most revealing and influential are *Ajoblanco* (Barcelona: first issue May 1974), *Ozono* (Madrid) and *El viejo topo* (Barcelona).

galvanised by reaction to the 'Ley de peligrosidad social y rehabilitación social' ('Law on Threats to Society and Social Rehabilitation').[4] This, the main legitimiser of repression of homosexuals in Spain, had been introduced on 4 August 1970, and modified and slightly liberalised the existing 'Ley de Vagos y Maleantes' ('Law on Vagrants and Malefactors'), but in a further modification on 1 June 1971 made specific provision for the internment of homosexuals in a 'rehabilitation centre' at Huelva, thus reverting almost to the same degree of severity of the previous law (which had, since 1954, specified labour camps).[5] A manifesto of the same year, attributed to the Frente de la Liberación Homosexual del Estado Español, called for far-reaching liberalisations which might lead to 'the recognition by society of the inalienable right of every human being freely to do with their own body what they wish'.[6]

Villena's first essay on counter-cultural politics, *La revolución cultural: Desafío de una juventud* (*The Cultural Revolution: The Challenge of a Young Generation*), came out in 1975, while the dictator was still alive, and it takes for granted a considerable degree of sexual-political awareness in its readership. So too does another essay published in 1975, *Gay Rock* by Eduardo Haro Ibars (1948–88), who was to become a close friend and admirer of Villena's. This is an anarchic but thorough-going reinscription into Spanish culture of the transgressions and energy of rock culture (particularly Glam Rock) and 1970s gay politics. At one stage it

4. For an account of Spanish studies of homosexuality published in the 1970s, see Smith, *Laws*, pp.4–8; for a basic history of gay liberation in the West, see Jeffrey Weeks, *Coming Out: Homosexual Politics in Britain from the Nineteenth Century to the Present*, London, 1977, Part Five, pp.185–237. In addition to the studies examined by Smith, see Ernesto Cadena, *Los marginales*, Barcelona, 1978, which is particularly informative on the growth of the new radical groupings, and Héctor Anabitarte and Ricardo Lorenzo, *Homosexualidad: el asunto está caliente*, Madrid, 1979. Both these emphasise the awareness of current debates around sexual politics within Spain, and especially Catalunya, in the period 1968–74. Anabitarte and Lorenzo make their points under the section heading 'España no es diferente' ('Spain Isn't Different') (p.18), though suggesting that only after Franco's death did 'homosexuals come out onto the streets' (p.70) (see also Smith, *Laws*, p.3 and note). On the `Ley de peligrosidad . . .', see Antoni Mirabet i Mullol, *Homosexualidad hoy: ¿Aceptada o todavía condenada?*, Barcelona, 1985 (trans. of the original Catalan *Homosexualitat avui*, Barcelona, 1984), pp.164–6.
5. Mirabet i Mullol, *Homosexualidad*, p.164. All references to homosexuality were removed from the law on 26 December 1978 (see Mirabet, p.166).
6. Reproduced in Alfonso García Pérez, *La rebelión de los homosexuales*, Madrid, 1976, pp.40–3.

links 'Quevedo, Genet and Burroughs: *pícaros,* rent boys and transvestites',[7] thus matching Villena's own approach to the Franco years, which was to combine this kind of radical combination of diverse elements with denials and subversions of the normalising processes of the régime and of its cultural icons.

Constructions of areas of micro-resistance to the régime abound in his short stories and in *In Front of the Mirror,* and dissidence is brought right to the heart of the dominant social structures. In 'The Portrait on the Bedside Table' from *For the Turkish Gods (Dioses turcos,* pp.107–14), it is the family which is disturbed by a form of (rather comfortable) libertarian resistance constructed out of the very materials of decent, bourgeois living – wealth, leisure and access to knowledge. This is the story of the narrator's Great Aunt Marcela. At the start we learn that he remembers her in 1960 or 1961 when 'she said nothing at all about Spanish current affairs' (p.107), and later when 'she cut herself off completely from the flat mediocrity of life in post-war Spain' as part of her heroic determination to 'keep her mask on at the party', knowing that 'her time was over' (p.113). In doing this she was not alone but part of one of Villena's favoured groups of dissidents, social and literary. (As Villena says in an interview reviewing the poetry of his friends and contemporaries during the last years of the régime, 'our protest against Francoism was precisely to ignore it'.)[8] Like the sometimes haughty Cernuda on the subject of Spain in his lifetime, her dissidence shades easily into exclusivist snobbery:

> Mi tía (¡qué personaje tan arcáico y tan nuevo parece ahora!) pertenecía a un mundo [...] cortés, festivo, [y] aunque estuviese en su país se sentía ajena ante lo rudo, lo elemental, lo productivo, ante – quiero imaginar – esas manifestaciones toscas a las que ha sido tan asidua la grey española . . . (p.113)

> My aunt (what an archaic and yet what a novel personality she now seems!) belonged to a [...] courteous and festive world [and] even if living in her own native Spain she felt herself to be above all that was coarse and raw, all that was productive, above – as I like to imagine she would think – the crass obviousness that the Spanish herd so often and so assiduously displays . . .

7. Eduardo Haro Ibars, *Gay Rock,* Madrid, 1975, p.93.
8. Interview with Antoni Munné, 'El clasicismo como novedad', in *Quimera,* no. 13 (November 1981), pp.21–3: 'nuestra protesta contra el franquismo consistía justamente en ignorarlo' (p.23).

The snobbery – readers of Villena come to learn – is not to be taken straight, however, but as an inverse statement, allowing elitist sympathies certainly, but equally meaning to recalibrate the values behind them by shocking the reader out of supposing flatly that here is another straightforward middle-class liberal or leftist. Spanish readers will not be so surprised: similarly direct and uncompromisingly exclusivist in their analyses of orthodox Spanish society under Francoism are Cernuda and the novelist Juan Goytisolo (b.1931).

In the later *Boys* resistance is more active and political positions more clearly readable. The early part of the story 'Peter' (*Chicos*, pp.11–39) is concerned with placing events in a context constructed out of the political, the personal and the historical. The words which bind the three parts of the story are 'liberty', 'experience' and 'modern' (pp.13–16). The narrator (who sometimes nearly is but who also is certainly not Luis Antonio de Villena himself) is just starting out at university, seventeen that October, fresh from his 'absurd Catholic school' (p.12), going into a student world where

> *Lucha* fue uno de los términos predilectos. El segundo, quizá, *huelga activa*. Mayo del '68 (inmediato, palpable) era puro presente, futuro casi. Nada parecido a una entelequia muerta. Todo resultaba y se quería *social*. Y cada mañana *Mundo Obrero* (el periódico clandestino del PCE) aparecía, como por magia, encima de nuestros pupitres. (p.13)

> *Struggle* was one of the favoured terms. The other most obvious one, perhaps, was *strike action*. May '68 (immediate and palpable) was right there before us, present, so near that it almost seemed it was yet to come. Not at all like a long-dead entelechy. Everything either was or was made to be a *social issue*. And every morning *Mundo Obrero* [*Workers' World*] (the clandestine newspaper of the Communist Party of Spain) would appear as if by magic on our desktops.

Even as the text is busy emphasising the importance of organised politics the narrator is disowning it: 'I could not fully feel I was a communist, nor did the word *commitment* appeal to me' (p.13). Only out of difference is he able retrospectively to construct a code of taste and behaviour, taking the word *libertad* (*liberty*) – italicised like *strike action* and *commitment* and therefore emphatically like them – and remaking it to form a sign of resistance which effectively will distance him from such keywords of conventional political struggle:

soñaba con un país democrático, libre, inflamado de vida – cual lo había palpado en mis viajes a Francia y lo comprobaría aún mejor – pero era el territorio de la libertad misma y no el de la política, el que a mí íntimamente me apetecía explorar, al parecer – hube de decirme – contra la mayoría. Para mí *libertad* era una palabra moral y conllevaba la transgresión del horizonte cotidiano. Sentía que esa *libertad*, entre otras materias, rozaba el cuerpo, abría los portones que la mente le cerraba a éste, y convirtiendo a cada individuo en un ser *único*, en un personaje singular y realizado, permitía después unirse solidariamente a los demás convertidos en individuos, en próximos, y nunca en *masa*. Probablemente no llegaba entonces a un razonamiento afilado o silogístico, pero ése era mi sentir exactamente. [...] Buscaba una libertad más íntima o más honda, no desdeñaba la acción (aunque la entendiese de otra manera) pero sin saber, torpemente, a tientas, anhelaba **experiencia**. No necesitaba las rojas soflamas sociales para sentirme libre, precisaba un camino más sutil, más interior, más oscuro, más inquietante y de trastorno. (pp.13–14)

I dreamt of a free, democratic country, full of the fire of life – just as I had glimpsed it in my trips to France, and later was to come to know more fully – but it was the sphere of freedom proper and not that of politics which I most deeply wanted to explore; apparently quite unlike the majority – as I had also to recognise.

For me *liberty* was a moral word and it implied transgressing the boundaries of everyday experience. I felt that this *liberty*, amongst other things, touched on the body and opened the portals shut against it by the mind, and by making each individual *unique*, a singular and complete personality, it allowed one then to become united in solidarity with others, themselves made into individuals, fellow men, and never part of the *masses*. Probably I had not in those days arrived at a finished, logical analysis, but this was exactly my sense of it. [...] I was looking for a deeper or more personal kind of liberty, I did not disdain active involvement (even if by it I understood something else) but without fully knowing it, clumsily feeling my way towards it, what I desired was **experience**. I had no need of the flaming red banners of social involvement to feel free, I required a subtler, more inward path, a darker, more disturbing and disruptive path.

This is an interesting mix of classic reactionary thought in the first set of adjectives up to 'dark [darker]' (the kind of thought which ascribes social unrest to spiritual need) and of revolutionary thinking in the second set ('darker' belonging to both discourses). The shake-up the narrator had and has in mind represents a real threat to the *status quo*. The link between transgression (of the boundaries of everyday experience) and the body, and the rereading of the notion of liberty as 'making each individual *unique*' but 'united in solidarity with others', makes this gesture individualist in Wilde's sense as read by Dollimore: 'less to do with a spiritual essence [...] than a social potential [...] both a desire for a radical *personal freedom* and a desire for *society itself* to be radically different' (Dollimore, *Sexual Dissidence*, pp.8–9). On the other hand, transgression, as Elizabeth Wilson suggests, is not *'per se* radical. Historically it has been linked with fascism as well as left wing politics, or is perhaps more likely to lead to an apolitical dandyism';[9] and libertarianism risks being just 'ideas in the void'.[10]

The essay 'La contracultura' ('Counter-culture'),[11] published in 1982 and thus representing a position between that of the narrative present of 'Peter' (1989) and the days of the student politics portrayed (the early 1970s), avoids the apolitical risk, at least at the surface of explicit statement. The politics is, however, revisionary and in a sense perverse. It wants both to transgress and still to value established culture, to put a scandalous edge to it but reaffirm it. Villena is careful to distance himself from any revolutionary implications in the term *contracultura* which in the Spanish sounds more obviously as if it is 'against' culture than perhaps it does in English: 'it is not something set *against* culture ('no algo *contra* la cultura) [...] rather a cultural movement itself set against the established system and dominant social values of the time' (p.90). Better, he suggests, to use the terms *'fringe culture'* (*'cultura marginal'*), *'new culture'* or 'at least *a culture against the grain'* (*'cultura a la contra'*) (p.90). Also he wants to apply the term much more widely than Theodore Roszak in his *The Making of A Counter Culture* (1968), cited by Villena early in the essay:[12] this is more than a Californian phenomenon of the 1960s for Villena, it is 'a constant of history: the will towards an optimistic kind of marginalisation, that ever possible search for happiness here and now, on earth, the

9. Elizabeth Wilson, in her contribution to the forum/chapter 'Transgression or chicken shit?' in Cherry Smith (ed.), *Lesbians Talk Queer Notions*, London, 1992, p.46. Dollimore, in his discussion of *The Well of Loneliness*, also worries that 'transgressive appropriations [of dominant codes and negative representations] are, from another perspective, reactionary alignments' (*Sexual Dissidence*, p.50).
10. 'Libertarianism as Ideas in the Void' is the title of a 1973 article by Wilson, in Elizabeth Wilson and Angela Weir (eds), *Hidden Agendas: Theory, Politics, and Experience in the Women's Movement*, London, 1986, pp.42–50.
11. In Fernando Savater and Luis Antonio de Villena, *Heterodoxias y contracultura*, Barcelona, 1982, pp.87–157.
12. The Spanish translation, by Angel Abad, *El nacimiento de una contracultura*, was published in 1972 by Kairos, Barcelona.

lasting desire to be comrades (intimately too) and to be free' (p.90). For Villena this new culture rereads and rewrites the decadents of the *fin-de-siècle*, the surrealists and the Tao-te-ching, Alesteir Crowley and the goliards of the Middle Ages, Ginsberg's 'Howl' and the haiku, so that again it is a process of transculturation as much as of rebellion.

It is in his discussion in 'Counter-culture' of the emergence of radical groupings in North America and Western Europe post-1969 (pp.140–2) that Villena comes closest to an alignment with contemporary leftist sexual politics and closest to a straightforward gay discourse; but there are instabilities. There is a slippage through the text from talk of *'Gay Power'*, *'radical groups'* and *'the gay liberation front'* to the much tamer statement, immediately following on from this last, that 'what these groups have achieved since 1969 in such an area of injustice as that of homosexual discrimination (sic: 'la discriminación homosexual') has been considerable' (p.141). The English term *'Women's lib'* is used directly as synonymous with the feminism of 1969 and of 'today' (i.e. shortly before publication in 1982), thus eliding huge changes and differences and either unconsciously or consciously ignoring the dismissive connotations of classic brute anti-feminism that have emerged from the term. Early 1980s feminism is seen as 'representing' (merely):

> las *Women's lib*, las *feministas,* representan hoy una forma muy activa de la lucha por la emancipación de la mujer y por el acercamiento entre los sexos (en lo que coinciden con los *gay*), para que lo masculino y lo femenino no sean infranqueables barreras, sino actitudes de una común manera de *ser humano.* (p.141)

> a highly active form of struggle for women's emancipation and a narrowing of the gap between the sexes (and here their aims are the same as those of gays), so that the masculine and the feminine are no longer uncrossable barriers but instead different attitudes to the common business of *being human.*

At just this point, where we expect the essay to adopt fully an essentialist position and invoke explicitly Human Nature, the direction changes interestingly: 'the differences (not genetic differences) which people have wanted to see between masculinity and femininity are not natural – as they would have us believe – but *cultural'* (p.141). There is then much unresolved tension in Villena's counter-cultural project at this stage.

The section 'Comunas, alternativas a la pareja, nuevas relaciones' (pp.136–7: 'Communes, Alternatives to Monogamy, New Relationships') also displays a familiarity with some of the key ideas of leftist sexual political analysis and we can see a nascent anti-heterosexist discourse. There is too, for the first time in the whole essay, a willingness to abandon the dry mix of academic and reporting style imposed by the volume's original aims and scope: there is now more involvement and more convolution. The *'new* family' of alternative living is set against the 'rigid scheme' of 'the basic model of a male-female couple, geared, what is more – following the Judeo-Christian model – to procreation and the patriarchal family' (p.136). The difficulties, 'the tensions and friction' of communal living make 'the ideal commune [...] seem very remote to us today'.

> But it is a consolation to think that the more traditional couple would have similar difficulties (and do) were it not that they are backed by centuries of trying out this basic scheme and putting it into practice, which no doubt creates in individuals a deep predisposition towards this type of relationship (the boy who thinks about getting a girlfriend without anyone really explaining to him what this might mean), a *predisposition* which moralists are then able happily go on to confuse with *nature* ('una *predisposición* que los moralistas luego confundirán muy gustosos con *naturaleza*'). (p.137)

There are again distinctly un-radical currents in this section on the communal alternative. The alternative sting is taken out of the tail by the assertion in parenthesis that the idea of the commune 'contains, naturally, a considerable dose of idealism' (p.136). So it is, more comfortably, poetic; and even, in that apologetic twist beloved of closet conservative pragmatists and sensible fathers, unrealistic. Similarly there is a liberal humanist strain in the analysis of the idea of communal living and the creation of the alternative family (itself far from being an obviously radical concept):

> The idea of the commune [...] does not only imply – as its detractors have wanted to stress – collective sexual experience, but human intercourse where things held by traditional society to be unpleasant shift to the more accepted level of the natural ('pasan al aceptado rango de *naturales*'). So the commune can mean the negation of taboos about bodily odours, can be about the absolute normality of the body's reactions and needs, things which there is no reason to hide, and so on . . . (p.136)

There is no previous textual evidence to imply or directly say that Villena is reusing 'natural' and 'normality' transgressively or imputing a transgressive use of the terms to those living the alternative. This radical turn is (perhaps) yet to come in his textual career. Radical enough though is his brief, and parenthetical, extension of the discussion to homosexuality within a fragment of the text which represents the beginnings of a critique of heterosexism and binary oppositional discourse:

> but the commune – in one or other of its manifestations – is not the only alternative to the traditional couple offered by the counter-culture. By imagining and wanting relationships based on understanding, on the breaking of taboos, on mutuality in friendship and not just on the masculine-feminine duality, a kind of friendship may emerge which perhaps will not see the body as a barrier (thus overcoming the absurd and mimetic assignment of sex roles in homosexual couples ('la absurda y mimética distribución de la pareja homosexual por roles sexuales'); we might see three-way relationships, matriarchal family structures or open ones, or indeed any other means of promoting free and affectionate bonding. (p.137)

In *Boys* and a number of the short stories such possibilities are explored: in fictions Villena charts his own sentimental education, vividly sketches in a gay counter-culture, and dramatises the difficulties of coming into full awareness of the politics (or, as Villena would prefer to say, ethics) of radical living. There is little doubt as to where his poetic voices and narrators stand in relation to heterosexism, patriarchy, moral prescriptiveness, decency and family values but the writing itself continues to be stimulatingly equivocal and undecidable. In a poetic manifesto written in 1974, 'El poema esboza al hombre' (in *Hymnica, Poesía*, pp.154–5: 'The Poem Is The Outline of The Man'), Villena expresses his loathing of conformity:

> Sí, yo aborrezco [...]
> La gente cuyos días no esgrimen sentimientos.
> Quien se abandona al río, no como el nadador,
> sino cual piedra. Detesto a la gente que
> hace de sus pasos un círculo continuo.
> Quien deja su noche caer tras la cortina,
> o busca la dócil fatuidad de un placer doméstico.

> Yes, I loathe [...] people whose days do not engage with feelings. / Those who surrender to the river not as a swimmer does / but as a stone. I detest those who make / of their steps a continuous circle. /

Who allow their nights to fall behind closed curtains, / or seek the tame fatuity of some domestic pleasure.

But Villena's writing – graceful and convoluted, measured and outrageous, sensual always – and the sheer pace of the lives represented and the dynamics of the attitudes invented are all designed to save us from sinking like the hateful stone to the dreary depths. The 'tame fatuity of [...] domestic pleasure' is resisted and private lives are made to turn about transgression.

In the story 'La íntima historia de una dama de mundo' ('The Private History of A Woman of the World' in *For the Turkish Gods*) (*Dioses turcos*, pp. 75–89) the protagonist lives a life in the leisured pursuit of beauty and boys:

> Para mí fue siempre una amiga de mamá [...] que acudía algunas tardes a tomar el té, y charlaba de muchas cosas moviendo delicadamente las manos, y adoptando una postura al sentarse, tan perfecta y eurítmica, de tanto *estilo* según se suele decir, que me cautivaba en tal modo que intentaba imitarla cuando estaba en mi cuarto a solas. (p.75)

> To me she was always a friend of mamma's [...] who would come to the house on some evenings to drink tea and would talk about any number of things, delicately moving her hands and sitting with so perfect and harmonious a posture, with such *style*, as they say, that I was captivated; so much so that I would try to imitate her when I was alone in my room.

She is associated with the narrator's sentimental education but if she is read just as serving as a role model to the artist as a young boy then a rather crude typology of gay development emerges. What is interesting is the narrator's own attention to the surface of her story and to '*style*' as a marker of difference as well as of affinity:

> En casa, y a próposito de ella, se hablaba siempre de su elegancia, de su buen tono, con el que nos sentíamos unánimes y con el que encantaba, pero también, debo decirlo, de sus rarezas, de sus extraños caprichos, de sus aventuras insólitas, que si para mi padre revestían un aura antipática, para mamá – tan amiga suya – eran disculpables como algo más de su forma de vida, de su singularidad, de su encanto. (pp.75–6)

> At home, when she was talked about, it was always her elegance, her refinement which were mentioned, and we were unanimous on this and this it was which most charmed us; but also mentioned, I have to say, were her peculiarities, her strange whims and extraordinary

adventures, which while they represented for my father something he disliked, for mamma – such a close friend – they were forgivable as being just another part of her way of life, her individuality, her charm. So a perception of difference through surface style folds nicely into a politics of the family, the naive version of which (that upheld by the father) purports to be upholding deeper, more serious, values. Mother, son and elegant lady form a sisterhood of radical frivolity; father is implicated as the gruff philistine, so straight that where they see elegance he sees 'too much make-up' and that 'when the talk was of her little acts of dissidence father continued to frown and must even, I suppose, have thought her depraved' ('una perversa') (pp.76 and 84).

The vital source of her dissidence is revealed to the narrator as sexual. He hears from his mother of her friend:

> Claro que era sensible a la belleza [...] y *a toda la belleza*, recalcó. Y entonces me contó otras cosas que yo había oído rumorear en cenas y reuniones. Mi elegante dama de mundo, con la maravillosa esmeralda entre los dedos largos, bebía mucho algunas noches, y salía a la calle en busca de chicos guapos. Le encantaban los muchachos. No desconocía ciertas esquinas, ciertos bares, en horas de la noche, sobre todo. Y mamá sabía de cheques con buenas sumas, para hacerse acompañar unas vacaciones por el chico aquel ¿recuerdas?, le decía, aquél que parecía un dios griego y es hermoso, hermoso . . . (p.80)

> Of course, she was sensitive to beauty [...] and, she emphasised, to all sorts of beauty. And she then told me other things which I had heard rumoured at various dinners and parties. My elegant woman of the world, with that fabulous emerald on her long fingers, on some evenings drank a good deal and would go out in search of good-looking boys. She loved teenage boys. She was no stranger to certain street-corners and bars, in the small hours above all. And mamma knew of cheques made out for considerable sums of money to have that boy accompany her on a holiday, do you remember? (she would say to her), the one who looked like a Greek god and is so lovely to look at, lovely . . .

This handsome boy picked up in Naples, with his classical name (Tulio) and 'dressed in a shirt which looked like a sailor's, and in tight trousers' (p.81) is an icon around which an entire alternative cultural practice forms, within the controlling purlieus of elegance. When he dies – in a classic movie-style plummet off a cliff into rocks and flames – and when she fades away – icy-handed and sipping on fortified champagne – the two of them, paradoxically and perversely, make their escape from social convention by being inserted into the strong cultural conventions of glamorous fictions of decline and fall. In the terms of the text, they have to die to escape the social death of the flat, controlling common sense of patriarchy.

The most explicit treatment of moral control within the patriarchal model takes the form of a short story in the tradition of nineteenth-century realism, spiced with tart social observation and telling detail. This is the ironically named 'Comentarios reales' (pp.19–29: 'Royal Commentaries'). The 'commentaries' in question are those made by the neighbours in a block of Madrid apartments about the sudden departure, and the behaviour, of 'the man on the fourth floor', as he is known, a distinguished single gentleman with a taste for art and enjoyment. The blindnesses of decent society here are many and amusing. The church-going widow Doña Amalia Tárregui (on the fifth floor) who accosts the man one day in his apartment for a donation to parish funds sees but does not understand the significance of 'the head from a polychrome wood statue, the head of an angel, a blond Saint Michael' (p.23). The presence of the angel is a sign no non-heterosexual would be likely to miss in the physical surroundings of the apartment (very grand and very cluttered and very Arty), confronted with a man who at two in the afternoon is dressed in 'a lovely silk dressing gown in fuchsia' (p.22). She is puzzled by the context but charmed by him (perhaps not least because he offers her a 5,000 peseta cheque out of politeness), remembering – after he has left the apartment-block in mysterious circumstances – how she had 'seen pictures of him every now and again in magazines – with theatre people; always in the background of course, which if anything makes him even more distinguished' (p.23). The revelation which comes at the end of the story also comes in photographic form. Jaime, the pompous and moralistic Doctor Ignazar's seventeen-year-old son, sees the 'man on the fourth floor' leaving the building for the last time, and in a hurry. The man drops some papers on his way out of the door, and Jaime sees them when he goes back down:

> vio dos papeles cuadrados. Los recogió en seguida, y su primera idea fue salir corriendo a entregárselos a su dueño [...] Pero entonces miró las fotos – eran dos fotos – y se quedó parado. Un chico de su edad, o algo mayor – en una – con el cuerpo fornido y un mechón de pelo cayéndole por la frente, estaba tumbado, casi desnudo, sobre la arena de una playa. Sonriente, retador, como desafiante. En la otra, ese mismo muchacho, sonriente también, y en traje de marinero ahora –

la gorra sostenida en una mano – pasaba un brazo por el hombro del señor que acababa de salir, el *señor del cuarto*. Alrededor la soleada terraza de un café, y al fondo, el mar feliz de un día de verano. (p.29)

he saw two square pieces of paper. He picked them up at once, and his first thought was to run after their owner and give him them. But then he looked at the photographs – which is what they turned out to be – and was stopped in his tracks. A boy of his own age, or a bit older – in one of them – well-built, with a lock of hair falling down over his forehead, was lying almost naked on the sand on a beach. Smiling, defiant, almost challenging. In the other, the same boy, smiling again and dressed now in a sailor's uniform – the cap in his hand – had his arm around the shoulders of the man who had just now left the building, the man on the fourth floor. Around them, the sunlit terrace of a café, and in the background the radiance of the sea on a summer's day.

The pompous and puritanical doctor indirectly gets his come-uppance as his son gazes at these images, and the inhabitants – the commentators – are quite brutally repositioned, in a sudden shift of perspective. The block of apartments becomes just so many dark and blinkered realms set far off from life as it really is and removed from pleasure, light, happiness – and from the boy on the beach.

Coming Out and Getting Away: Transgression as Travel

In 'Peter' the sixties, hippy culture and rock music play an important part in involving the book in the discourse of history and in conforming the narrator's sense of sexuality and liberation. Madrid is established, in the years immediately preceding Franco's death, as a city whose culture is defined by reference outwards. Peter himself is exotic (Lithuanian-born with Canadian nationality). The literary and artistic interests of the three refined buddies, the narrator, José Ignacio and Peter, are emphatically unpatriotic, mostly non-contemporary, and eclectic: Poe, Baudelaire, Nerval, Huxley; Somerset Maugham, Alesteir Crowley, Lord Dunsany, Arthur Machen, Saki, Lovecraft, Jean Ray; Balthus, Gilles de Rais and art deco (*Chicos*, pp.14–23). The narrator travels to see Peter and Jose in London and Deia (on Mallorca); Peter, in a rapid moral decline, goes to California, then (on the hippy trail) to India where, in a narratorially-imposed supreme symbolic act of separation from Madrid and from cultural contact, he loses first his voice and then his memory.

Much of the response to Peter's personal interpretation of liberation depends on the narrator's two trips out of Madrid in 1970 to visit Peter and Jose, in the Spring to London and in August to Mallorca. Peter has a relationship with a Greek woman called Ilona in London (where he and Jose have gone to live for a while, in search of the legacy of the 1960s) in a flat full (according to the narrator's observations on a visit there) of marijuana, Henry Miller, *The Perfumed Garden*, old rancid milk bottles, Colin Wilson and acid (pp.28–9). Peter and Ilona have noisy sex everywhere and in front of everyone: 'It was all the same to Peter whether he walked in with an erection or started to warm her up while we were talking or eating' (p.29). Heterosexuality has a major and revealing part to play in the argument of the decline and fall of what the narrator holds as supreme values, but he is by no means fixedly unorthodox and his sexuality occupies a number of unreconciled positions. There is an interesting ambivalence whereby, while ostensibly looking back on a previous unreconstructed morality, the narrator reveals a persistence of its control over him. On the day he is due to leave London he goes to Peter's bed:

> y espié las sábanas siempre revueltas, pues allí nadie hacía las camas. Me pareció ver muchas manchas de semen o de jugos sexuales, y noté una mezcla de atracción y asco. Pasé, tocando, los dedos por encima, y en seguida corrí al lavabo a limpiarme y volví a mis bultos. (p.30)

> and I looked at the sheets – disordered as always, since nobody ever made the beds there. I thought I saw lots of stains on them from semen or sexual juices, and I felt a mixture of attraction and disgust. I ran my fingers over the sheets, touching them. And at once I ran to the bathroom to wash and went back to my packing.

This, the rawness and prudishness of the sexually undeclared and domestically still unweaned, is also a complex phobia, especially in that nice bourgeois detail, the concern for unmade beds: a sexuality recoiling from heterosexual practices but also a homosexuality seeing itself as Other (as unruliness, as, indeed, sex) and running off appalled to pack its bags.

The flaunting of heterosexual desire in 'Peter', with all the obviousness of the erection which is seen so often around the flat, marks the cruel distance that separates the narrator from the subtleties once seemingly promised by the comradeship of the three men. Ordinary desire points nowhere: 'on another occasion, walking to a bookshop with Jose, I asked him about Peter. I would have said that he had *lost his way*, but I kept quiet since it sounded a very bourgeois thing to say' (p.29). At the time of telling, though, he does not suppress the word and there is a clear sense that the objective of Jose's and the narrator's walk, to look at or buy books, is being set against Peter's lack of direction. Better a nice cultured walk to a Hampstead bookshop (for Hampstead it is where Peter and Jose are slumming it) than free love all over the kitchen. The narrator's own rather conventional purpose in visiting London, after all, was 'to see the pre-Raphaelites and look for books on the Decadents' (p.27).

Peter, according to Jose, is in search of his true self through sex and drugs – very much in the tradition of the early 1970s – and the narrator admits that

> Había muchas cosas en todo aquello que hallaban mi asentimiento (el culto a la experiencia misma, la bohemia) pero me aterraba el desorden. [...] Follar y drogarse no me parecía mal, de entrada, pero intuía que Peter (bajo sus ansias místicas) no llegaría a ninguna parte. (p.29)

> There was a lot I could identify with in all this (the cult of experience itself, bohemianism) but disorder terrified me. [...] Fucking and drugs didn't seem bad to me *per se*, but my intuition told me that Peter (under the influence of his mystical preoccupations) was going nowhere.

Peter's end, after a period of mysticism- and drug-induced indigence in India, is seen as 'a pathetic story which enlightens us, perhaps, as to the unfailingly dreadful dangers that await those who stray from the path' (p.39) and the end of his story is allegorised, with him arriving 'at the gates of death through malnutrition, and sailing fulfilled and sweetly weightless through a galaxy which is the Universal Woman' (p.39). The allegory is deliberately undermined both by the shades of Miller in the symbolism of heroic, heterosexual conquest and by the narrator's descriptions of the earlier stages in the journey, already marked out as a non-journey. Peter's transgression has doubled back on itself to become obviousness.

Similarly, when living in California, Peter becomes 'obsessed with sex', according to Jose, and, *'not the same'* (p.33):

> Decidió que la pasión era lo único que contaba en la vida, lo único que te hace sentir vivo, aunque frente a tan fácil verdad añadió – tras la

lectura de cuatro libros divulgatorios y coloristas sobre hinduismo – que ese arrebato (el del sexo) no sólo enaltece y exacerba la vida sino que es, por más, el camino que nos pone en íntimo y definitivo contacto con el universo. Para Peter el universo, con su tentadora y terrible inmensidad, llena de siglos luz y de agujeros negros, debía ser – era – una tremenda acogedora vagina en cuya sima – algún día – concluiríamos diluyéndonos o integrándonos, llenos de gozo. (p.33)

He [Peter] decided that passion was the only thing that counted in life, the only thing that made you feel alive, although to such an easily discovered truth he added – having read a couple of popularist and colourful books on Hinduism – that the special ecstasy (of sex) not only heightens and sharpens life but, more than that, it is the path which puts us in closer and more lasting contact with the universe. For Peter, the universe, in all its tempting and terrible immensity, full of light years and black holes, must have been – it was – an awesome, welcoming vagina in whose abyss – one day – we would all end up, dispersed or integrated with it, and full of joy.

It is fairly clear that all these things – the 'truth' about life, pseudo-Hinduism and nostalgia for the womb – are seen as equally absurd from the point of view of the narratorial present (although, as ever, the text displays a perverse delight in the description, at the end of this paragraph, of the beauty of decline and annihilation).

The second of the narrator's own escapes from Madrid, the visit to Deia, serves as another reminder that the cultural and sexual *transición* in Spain was alive and well some years before Franco's death, at least in separated pockets of resistance and for the moneyed classes. (In *Amour Passion*, Ibiza, Menorca, Benidorm and Marbella are also alluded to as long-established hot spots of sexual unorthodoxy: *Amor pasión*, pp. 31 and 67.)[13] The episode is also used to continue the fond description of the absurdities of hippy mysticism and heterosexual mythifications of desire. The village is 'plagued with exotic foreigners. Women with curly hair in flowered skirts, all rags and tatters, little bells and amulets, and hennaed hair, no bra, hand-made sandals [...] And boys with very long hair' (p.31). The days go by in a frenzied haze of sex and drugs (though not for the narrator, who at this stage is still a virgin on

13. Best-selling novelist Manuel Vázquez Montalbán has written a neo-realist sketch, *Los alegres muchachos de Atzavara* (*The Fun-loving Boys of Atzavara*), Barcelona, 1987, set in a Catalan coastal resort and representing bourgeois homosexuality emerging from the closet of Francoism.

both counts). The presence of Robert Graves is used to underline again the value of books and a measured life as a necessary counterbalance (though not a substitute) to living life on the edge:

> Todos querían mucho al viejo Graves, cercano ya a la decrepitud total, al que vi un día en su jardín, silencioso, cargado de talismanes como un anciano y loco profeta, y cerrando tarros de miel que era de su cosecha. Pero imagino que él quería menos a estos *hipsters*, alguno probablemente pesado, y de los que se le sentía huir levemente. El amaba su Luna, su apartamiento, sus ensalmos, su privacidad, sus clásicos, su blanca musa druídica. Parecía coincidir con mis amigos. Pero pienso – hoy sobre todo – que era una coincidencia aparente. Mucho menos honda que colorista, menos real que codiciada por ellos. [...] Notaba – creía sentir – que todo aquel multicolor universo que se decía en rumbo a la plenitud de Acuario estaba compuesto por un cúmulo de hermosos y locos desnortados, que no iban a ningún sitio. Acaso no haya porqué ir a ningún sitio, es cierto. Pero yo sí deseaba ir a mi experiencia, a mi mundo – que no era ése – a mi transgresión, a mí mismo en definitiva, y así, aquello me rozaba tan sólo. Me apetecía, pero me rozaba, sólo eso. (pp.31–2)

Everyone was very fond of the elderly Graves, now near to complete decrepitude and whom I saw one day in his garden, laden with talismans like some mad, ancient prophet, silently sealing up pots of his own bees' honey. But I imagine that he was less fond of these *hipsters* than they of him, some of them being no doubt tedious; and you could see that, in a quiet way, he fled their company. His Moon, his apartment, his chants, his privacy, the classics, his white druidic muse, these were what he loved. He seemed to be like my friends. But I think, especially now, that it was only an apparent likeness, not so much deep-seated as superficially colourful, not so much real, more something they craved. He could see – as I thought I intuited – that this whole multi-coloured universe destined, as it declared, for the fullness of the age of Aquarius was made up of a collection of beautiful people and drifting madmen all going nowhere. Perhaps there's no reason to be heading in any direction, it's true. But I did want to move on, towards experience and my own world (this was certainly not it), towards transgression, my transgression, towards myself once and for all; and so all this only barely touched me. I liked the idea, but it only touched the surface, and that was all.

The narrator's relationship to the goings-on at Deia and, increasingly, to Jose and Peter is a sign of his and Villena's difference and dissidence. Even the most anti-establishmentarian culture available at the time falls short of his radical requirements, but also – because of the phobic complexity in the narrator – this culture problematises the very identity he thinks he is seeking. Deia is a dead-end: 'Deia meant days of wildness, days hastening on. Getting up very late, walks in the dark, nude bathing, cliffs and sloping hillsides, visions of sex – which I did not practise – and an endless psychedelic flight to the sound of the latest English and American rock bands' (p.31). Without desire, without insertion into gay culture, the narrator's is a multi-directional, hobbled flight from one set of unstable identities to another: from the pre-excursion narrator who is sensible conformist and restless dreamer, child of the family and wild, experimenting escapee towards a dissidence which turns out not to be one at all, where sexuality is a confusing trace on the sheets and desire is left without an identified or recognised object.

As Stephen Adams observes nicely of the symbolic stories of gay identification written prior to 1970: 'Nowadays [the] process is summed up in the gay liberation concept of "coming out", but in the past "going away" was the more likely starting point'.[14] Sexual acculturation is a flight, even an unknowing one, from predetermined social identities constructed by the state, the church, the family, the economic system, a search for new networks, a new dynamic, and this is recognised in many ways in Villena's texts. They also, however, discover that the retreat from the composite, symbolic home involves a move away from the library and the desk, from the established places of literary culture; and both these movements apparently away from the centre find themselves tracking back towards it to subvert it but also to undermine any straightforward aim of escaping into a counter-culture, coming out into the utopian light and finding a new identity. The movement of retreat and return, rather, questions and destabilises the old cultural and personal identities while nevertheless depending on them. The two following chapters continue to follow Villena through this movement of departure and tracking back, concentrating on the context of poetry and poetic tradition.

14. Stephen Adams, *The Homosexual As Hero In Contemporary Fiction*, London, 1980, p.56.

2

Retreat and Return

Forget Literature . . .

The novel *Beyond the World* chronicles the rebel anti-hero Álvaro's passage into oblivion and his progressive rejection of culture and of conventional counter-cultures (including drugs, drink and promiscuity diligently applied across most of the spectrum of sexual preference). He is fleeing from the death represented by stability in life. His dedication to excess is forged from a heady mix of Lautréamont, Ducasse, Poe, Nerval, Lou Reed, David Bowie, Mick Ronson, and Baudelaire (*Fuera*, pp.9–14 and *passim*), linked with manic depression, an infirm fatalistic idealism in the *fin-de-siècle* manner, an obsession with sensation and with moving on. But moving on makes him an outcast even from the unorthodox group of his friends, lovers and mentors.

A journey to North Africa with friends María and Carlos (who narrates for some of the novel) soon moves away from the relatively cosy dissidence of LSD-enhanced sex in Chauoen and exotic Marrakech with its lovely sunsets and precious exiles, one of whom, Maud Lenotre, epitomises leisure-class transgression in her love of liberty 'without shrill revolution' (p.54). The desert, as 'nothingness made flesh' (p.56), is Álvaro's special goal. By day the desert sun 'has, perhaps, the unbearable beauty of the angels' and reminds him of *The Book of the Dead* (p.57). By night (with more drugs) the three friends see 'star-emissaries of Death [...] the shimmering ice of the Stygian lake' (p.59). Álvaro's reading (with Paul Bowles now explicitly added to the list and Gide implied) has spread through the text, and when the three are at the Roman ruins of Volubilis he feels a 'dizzying sense of the infinite [...] that Bacchic sensation of being a part of all matter' and that he has become transformed 'into incandescent liquid' (p.73). Throughout the novel the late Romantic language of darkness, death and passion is Álvaro's realm.

Later, back in Madrid and having published a promising book of poems, established culture further alienates him. The literary crowd disgusts him ('he hated frivolity because it was not even frivolous': p.125) and he is disappointed even by a meeting with Aleixandre, the famous old man of Spanish letters, arranged by the not very clearly heterosexual scholar and lecturer Juan Ortín who is his mentor. Álvaro expects to meet 'the surrealist poet whose books he so loved [...] A subversive, a rebel, at odds with the world' (p.112). He expects, in fact, to meet the poet of *Pasión de la tierra*, a collection which Villena himself has linked to the 'infernal, visionary discourse' of Rimbaud and the radical linguistic adventures of Lautréamont ('Vicente Aleixandre', pp.65–76). Ideal for Álvaro, one might think:

> Pero habló a un viejo simpático, deliciosamente educado, con graves problemas en la vista, que le pidió que leyera algún poema de los que llevaba (él no podía hacerlo) y luego lo desmenuzó técnicamente con muy cortés generosidad. (*Fuera*, p.112)

> But in fact he spoke with an exquisitely civilised, kind old man with serious problems with his eyesight who asked him to read out one or other of the poems he had brought along (since he himself could not) and then analysed their technique with most courteous generosity.

Álvaro's determination to escape prompts another journey which this time is not to the symbolic desert but to the equally coded landscape of Sicily. Here, in the company of a completely directionless and radically unwashed young French boy Thierry – who is free from all reactions to art, culture, landscape and meaning – he gets closer to nihilistic amalgamation with the longed-for mud and dirt. He has sex with a filthy beggar named Gauguin. He and Thierry, urinating over each other in the ruins, look out beyond the monuments and sites towards imaginary 'ancient civilisations, prior to History, orgiastic and Pan-like in their nature' (p.144).

Beyond the World, in passages like this, empties out the meanings in culture as civilisation, making the splendours of ancient history, classical myth, or Western literature lose profound significance and gain a surface coding which Álvaro is keen to use as a guide to his own perpetual flight from identity, skating from one difference to another. The static and the monumental is death for him; true experience is a constant fragmentation and, in the end, his own ruination. But elsewhere in the book (and in his perceptions as relayed by the two narrators) his experience is very much in debt to the icons of high art and the grand narratives of literary culture. Álvaro's life, like that of so many of the protagonists of Villena's writing, is one invented at the intersection of culture and anti-culture, a location where to be an outlaw from one camp is always to belong almost in the other and to escape is to return.

Of the flagrantly escapist poem 'Excelentes proyectos de futuro' ('Excellent Plans for the Future') in *Poems on the Margins* Villena says 'I continue to think that one day I shall be its protagonist' (*Marginados*, p.10):

Ya sin escribir y con algún dinero, me iría
también de mi país huyendo de mí mismo.
Pasaría los días en ciudades de nombre fastuoso
y antiguo [...]
Y apoyando la soledad en las formas ilustres,
y el resto del deseo en los cuerpos pagados y bellísimos,
quizás me encontrase, al fondo de una noche, otro ser que hubo
en mí y que acabó perdiendo . . . [...]
La tarde dorará las colinas de Roma, celebérrimas,
o el nombre
hermoso del primordial Egeo,
mientras sentado en calma y en la terraza de algún hotel
de lujo, le estarás advirtiendo al joven compatriota de visita
(con gesto displicente y el daquirí tercero en la copa vacía)
– Olvídese, querido, olvide para siempre la literatura . . .

(p.18)

No longer writing, and with a little money put aside, I'd go away / fleeing from myself as well as from my country. / I'd spend the days in cities with resounding, / ancient names [...] / [...] / And helping loneliness along with the help of illustrious forms, / and what's left of desire with the help of bodies beautiful and bought, / perhaps I would meet in the depths of the night with another being who once there was / in me and who ended up the loser . . . / [...] / The evening will gild the celebrated hills of Rome, / or light the lovely name of the primordial Aegean, / while seated calmly on the terrace of some luxury / hotel, you'll be advising a young compatriot passing through / (with a disapproving look and the third daiquiri gone from the empty glass) / 'Forget literature, my dear, forget it for ever.'

Such studied urbanity writes this protagonist into the long history of weary flight from letters to sweet living with such obviousness that it destabilises what would otherwise be a straightforward myth of return to a more authentic self. What is imagined in these 'excellent plans' is the discovery (in sex and travel) of an alternative self remembered as one 'who loved so much and so well, and had a taste for art / without the vanities of works or monuments' (p.18: 'aquel vividor/ que tanto amó y tan bien, y gustó del arte/ sin vanidad de obra o monumento . . .'). However, the backdrops of Rome, the Aegean and a substantial hotel, and that embarrassing excess of daiquiris, offer little assurance of an imminent adoption of a more austere approach to life and art. And what more literary homosexual motif could there be than this affected retreat?[1]

While 'Excellent Plans for the Future' urges the abandonment of literature, another poem of retreat, 'Temas crepusculares' ('Twilight Themes') in *Death Alone* (*Poesía*, pp. 293–4) goes further and purports to turn its back on illusions as well. Here, instabilities and vulnerability are manifest beneath a mask of irony and tonal playfulness bordering on camp. Lost illusions are the main theme here, a grand old topic whose literary prestige is steadily eroded as the text advances:

> Las primeras ilusiones que se pierden
> (y hablo de sentimientos)
> mueven mucho aparato de tragedia,
> pero en realidad qué poco importa.
> El jersey roto se sustituye por uno nuevo aún mejor
> o cuando menos, y a nuestro parecer, aún más hermoso.
> La verdad es que en esos momentos
> la vida pugna por salir, el agua es clara, se cuela la ilusión
> (vivaz y alegre, aunque se derrumbe y vuelva)
> por todos los resquicios, por todas partes.
> Y el crepúsculo no es sino la esperanza de un día nuevo
> Pero después (lo sabes) es distinto.
> Se cruza el horizonte como sin darse cuenta.
> Se tacha un teléfono (o te cansa la voz)
> mas no hay con quien sustituirla. Y cuanto queda en lejanía,
> ese *te llamaré dentro de dos semanas*

---

1. Stephen Fry has recently investigated one aspect of the theme in an amusing introduction to a new edition of Norman Douglas's *Venus in the Kitchen*: 'the homosexual aesthete[s] brought up in Victorian England [...] disenfranchised and dispossessed by dint of their sexuality [...] took the offensive. Rather than inhabit a twilit world of shame in their homeland these men adopted the world, particularly the world of flesh, silk, light, ornament and detail [...] For Britons of a similar nature who do not possess the money, background, or literary flair, the usual course is to become a drag queen. Douglas, it might be said, wrote drag prose' ('Introduction' to Norman Douglas *Venus in the Kitchen*, ed. Fry, London, 1992, p.x).

que tú hubieses querido inminente y ahora,
saber que la novedad se vuelve cuesta arriba,
y que a menudo no se cambia el jersey
sino que se acude al arte muy pobre del remiendo;
todo eso te va llenando de nostalgia,
te va tornando irremisiblemente
más absurdo, más lejos [...]
has de decirte que ya no eres aquél,
te preguntas qué ha pasado, pues no hace aún mucho tiempo
y cuando intentas colocarte la vieja máscara,
no cabe, los rasgos no corresponden,
hay sutiles variaciones, pero definitivas e ineluctables.
Así es que sueñas quedarte en una isla,
empiezas a ser escéptico con el futuro,
te tiñes de añoranza, no te importa rebajarte
para pedir amor (*cariño*, acaso, que es palabra más débil)
aún esperando ya – y casi de antemano –
las dos inevitables semanas (perpetuas)
que habrá por medio. [...]
Y cuando los chicos se marchan de la isla, anocheciendo,
al que (como tú) pregunta si no es muy duro quedarse solo,
le respondes, sirviéndote una copa y con triste sonrisa,
esa frase que tanto has estudiado, esa frase tan tuya:
Querido, pero si todos estamos solos. ¿No lo sabes?

(pp.293–4)

The first illusions to be lost / (and here I speak of feelings) / put into
motion a whole paraphernalia of tragedy, / but in fact how very little
it all matters. / The sweater with a hole in it is soon replaced with a
newer and a better one / or at least, it seems to us, an even better-
looking one. / The truth is that in those moments / life is fighting to
break out, the water's clear, illusion seeps in / (lively and happy, even
if it turns again and falls) / to every corner, everywhere. / And the
twilight is but the hope of another day. / But later (as you know) it's
different. / The horizon is crossed without you knowing. / A phone
number's crossed out (or your voice fades) / but there's not another
there to take its place. And all those things which stay off in the
distance, / that *I'll call you within the fortnight* / which you would rather
think was imminent and now, / knowing that novelty's on the uphill
stretch, / and often the jersey cannot be changed / and one resorts to
the poor art of darning; / all this increasingly fills you with nostalgia,
makes you more and more / irredeemably absurd, more distanced /
[...] / and you have to say you are now not the one you were, / and
wonder what has happened, since it still was not all that long ago /
and when you try to put the old mask on, / it will not fit, the features

do not go, / there are subtle variations, but quite definitive, quite unavoidable. / And so it is you dream of staying on there on an island, / begin to have your doubts about the future, / become shot through with yearning, and don't mind stooping / to beg for love (or perhaps *affection*, as it's a weaker word) / while still expecting – and almost as if you knew beforehand – / the two (perpetual, inevitable) weeks / to wait between now and then. / [...] / And when the boys leave the island at nightfall / if anyone (like you) should ask if it isn't very hard to stay there on your own, / you say, and pour another drink with a sad smile, / that phrase which you've rehearsed so much, which is so much you: / *But, my dear, we are all alone. Didn't you know?*

This last theatrical phrase displays an important instability in the text: it is consciously hollow, clichéd, high-sounding, and pitiful. The speaker has a certain hint about him of a Somerset Maugham, Tennessee Williams or Noel Coward character; on the other hand the poet tells us in a deliberately ingenuous manner that this is a phrase that belongs specifically to him, and the use of the familiar second person *tú* does not distance us from the speaking subject, rather the opposite. We seem to know him much more intimately now, as if this were a private diary or an overheard confession. In italics, these words become associated on the page with those others '*I'll call within the fortnight*' and '*affection*'; these so ironically emphasised phrases have in common inauthenticity and the failure to fulfil the ideal. The poem ostensibly tells a story of disabusal: however, our narrator ends up learning nothing and the lesson of the masks and features which neither fit nor match is completely forgotten at the end. Where the island ought to be the ideal place of retreat for the newly-wise poet, far from the madding crowd, it is not a golden silence that is to be had here but the teasing humiliation instead of the silent telephone and the shrill affectation of that studied final line. The 'paraphernalia of tragedy' looked at askance at the start of the text has succeeded in infecting the whole. The weary voice and the crossed-out phone number are allegorical, like the torn, emotive sweater: all speak of failure, disconnection, the lack of wisdom and peace, of the shame of an imposed, not a chosen, resignation and retreat. Instead of the moment of erotic-linguistic epiphany familiar from other poems, where the carnal and the ideal fuse in a moment of ecstasy, here there is an insulting wait, a gap filled by neither fleshly nor spiritual fulfilments. There is an abyss stretched between the lyrical optimism of the early part of the poem and the realisation that 'all this [...] / makes you more and more irredeemably absurd, more distanced'. Crossing the horizon unknowingly is a reverse journey, not away from the self towards a better self but a return to a sad unstable centre. Going far away is not discovery, it is simply losing contact. And yet there is the pouring of another drink (signifying urbanity like the daiquiris in 'Excellent Plans for the Future') and there is that wry smile. By dramatising his own absurd isolation, the poet can feel somehow superior, set apart from his own apartness and far away, by means of this masquerade, from the part of his creative being which reveals itself to be debased in this same text. The simple sweater and silent telephone are talismans guarding against despair because they allow the theatricality as well as activating the allegory of decline. For such an exquisite *poseur* as the speaker here, his abandoned situation surely has a certain charm.[2] As Villena says in the prologue to *Poems on the Margins*: 'let nobody say at this late stage that success and marginalisation are incompatible' (*Marginados*, p.11). A Wildean transgressive remark which puts all the right people off the scent.

Dissident Mediterranean Culture

In the poem 'Madrid' (*Marginados*, p.21) the city is a sterile enclosing place, and it is used to set up a symbolic, contrastive geography. It is emptied of cultural meanings and even seems void of its customary pleasures:

Acaso tendré que estar siempre aquí,
no moverme nunca.
Bajo el sol abrasador del estío
y la glacial ventisca de un invierno largo.
Sin apenas leyendas, ni mitos, ni mar.
Yo que desearía una villa en Luxor,
habitar las playas de Sousse mucho tiempo,
recorrer la India, instalarme en Italia,
la feliz, la melancólica Italia . . .

(p.21)

2. For an earlier discussion of this poem in a slightly different context, see Perriam, 'Marginación y amor en la poesía de Luis Antonio de Villena', *Revista monográfica/Monographic Review*, vol. 7 (1991), pp.135–45.

Perhaps I shall have to be always here, / and never move. / Under
the burning summer sun / and the biting wind of a lengthy winter. /
With scarcely any legends, myths, or any sea. / I, who would like a
villa in Luxor, / to live for a long time on the beaches of Sousse, / to
travel through India, settle in Italy, / in smiling, melancholy Italy...

Such an Italy is a constant source of reference for Villena (which
should by now come as no surprise, given his credentials), as it was
for a number of poets of the late 1960s and early 1970s in Spain who
– frantically enriching poetry with both High and Popular Cultural
intertexts – more or less fit the literary historical category of *the
novísimos* (and some of whom, in fond or not so fond recognition
of one particular topographical obsession, were nicknamed the
venecianos, 'the Venetian poets'). Italy – the (then) rich relation –
seemed, or indeed was, especially sophisticated, culturally diverse
and free when seen from the perspective of Franco's increasingly
consumerist and tower-block-ridden Spain,[3] and from a literary
scene dominated by the more or less socially committed novel, by
a poetry still apparently moving between two fixed poles of tacit
political commitment and by verse heavy either with metaphysics
(famously, Jorge Guillén in his *Cántico*, Pedro Salinas and Juan
Ramón Jiménez) or a sentimental Catholic or Nationalist aesthetic.[4]

The cultural values attaching to the Italianate and, by extension,
the Mediterranean are overlaid in Villena by more specific though
interrelated interests: Neoplatonism, aesthetic theory and
homoeroticism; sculpture, architecture and fine art. The latter were
always part of the Italian package for the genteel traveller and
Villena unwraps it to find a glittering gift of sexual dissidence.
References to the statuesque and classical in relation to the male
form are popular stock in gay art from physique magazines to
poetry;[5] and there are many instances of highly coloured and

3. See John Hooper, *The Spaniards: A Portrait of the New Spain*, Harmondsworth,
1987, pp.24–34, on the 'economic miracle' and the growth of the major cities in
the 1960s.

4. See Butt, *Writers and Politics*, pp.39–48; also (more detailed, but in Spanish)
Carlos Blanco Aguinaga, Julio Rodríguez Puértolas and Iris M. Zavala, *Historia
social de la literatura española (en lengua castellana)*, vol. 3, Madrid, 1984, pp.84–9,
189–201 and 241–62.

5. The obsession is perhaps most obviously focused in fine art and in cinema,
and has been amusingly and sharply exploited in sequences in Constantine
Giannaris's *Caught Looking* (1991) which sends up the 'sensitive artistic' response
to the classical male pose while fondly demonstrating its potency. Giannaris is
himself consciously working in a tradition: see Richard Dyer, *Now You See It:*

framed set-pieces in Villena's earlier erotic poems, especially in *Hymnica* where strong backs, harmonious torsos, marble, bronze, reclining figures on divans and beds and the iconic Saint Sebastian are all to be seen, the latter in 'Día de sol en el rincón de un museo' ('A Sunny Day In A Corner of A Museum') (*Poesía*, pp.174–5). *Sublime Solarium* displays in exacerbated form the strategy of intense intertextual reference based around highbrow art and leisure which was a prime (and usually enriching) characteristic of the poetry of the *novísimos*, and *Hymnica* interlaces boys and art with considerable pace and intensity. Subsequently, however, Villena wishes to exceed and to disrupt such conventional cultural codings – including the gay ones – and to fragment the icons, especially those which are assimilable into what is probably most accurately called Grand Queen Culture. In the later writings, cosy cultural exoticism is troubled by a transgressive emphasis on the intersection of High Culture and less sanctified cultures, often through a wry, blatant sexiness or risky cross-associations which shatter the illusions of cultural stability and purity. So in '"David" por Donatello' ('Donatello's "David"') in *To Flee from Winter* (pp.206–7) the figure of David is eroticised by references to warmth, vibration, a copper skin and an arresting look which 'speaks with a pure peal of laughter of the bed chamber', and becomes 'the loveliest image of wickedness in the most nubile body' (p.207). It is made perverse, brought into the late Romantic era and into the world of homoeroticism. Similarly in 'Buonarroti' (*Death Alone*) 'sex is a forest / of abundance, the untellable passion of beautiful self-destruction' (p.32) and Michelangelo becomes by imputation one of the beautiful and the damned. (This impression is also given by the blurb of *I, Michelangelo*, a book described on its front cover as 'A portrait of Michelangelo the man: tormented, Neoplatonist, homosexual, scholar, aesthete, depressive', although the book's tone partly belies this sensationalism.)

The nostalgic, almost Proustian, poem 'Intento rehabitar la dicha' ('Once More I Try to Live in Happiness') in *Death Alone* (pp.310–15) is, within the seriousness of its intent, a thorough-going, joyful disruption of any merely solemn faith in old cultural values:

Studies on Lesbian and Gay Film, London, 1990, pp.63–74 and 129–34, on the films of Jean Cocteau and Gregory Markopoulos. Woods gives some of the very numerous examples from poetry in *Articulate Flesh*, pp.103–8.

Habíamos comido sandía al entrar en la ciudad,
aquel atardecer de un verano, junto a las murallas.
La noche cayó sobre una estatua del Dante
entre un aire suave y los trinos de Verdi o Donizetti . . .
[...]
la efigie del poeta bajo la inmensa luna,
los arcos, las *loggie,* las arias y su melodrama.
Y aquellos muchachos que querían llevarnos a un concierto
de *rock* . . .
Yo pensaba que el Amor vendría a asaltarme
en una esquina
[...]
Aquel Amor con la melena larga y camiseta Wrangler.

(pp.311–12)

We had sat eating water-melon when we entered the city, / that
summer evening, next to the city walls. / Darkness fell on a statue of
Dante / amid soft breezes and the trills of Verdi or Donizetti . . . / [...]
/ the poet's effigy under a giant moon, / the arches and loggias, the
arias and their melodrama. / And those boys who wanted to take us
off to a / rock concert . . . / I thought love would come and assault
me there / on the corner [...] / Love in the form of that boy with long
soft hair and a Wrangler tee-shirt.

A suspension of the metrical pattern and the lexical jolt caused
by the introduction of the rock concert mark out the thin line between a sense in Villena that this is absurd and a sense that this is
worth pausing on, worth italicising. Rock and Dante, sex and the
sublime, love in the ruins – the mix is a nice shake-up of sensibilit-
ies. Culture is getting reinscribed and homosexualised and into the
text is encrusted an epigram which reveals this reinscriptive act:

Y el viento, y su color y las palabras cultas,
y los jóvenes cuerpos, y la música leve,
y la promesa de una dicha con terrestre
sabor y carmesí, me repetían: Ama, suspira . . .

Ya que nunca volverás a ser joven como entonces,
pide a la música hoy que te devuelva a Verona

(p.312)

And the wind, and his colour and the cultured words, / and young
bodies, and the gentle music, / and the promise of a kind of happiness
with earthly / crimson flavour, repeated the words to me: Love, and
sigh . . . / Since you will never again be young as then you were, /
beg the music to return you today to Verona.

The key-phrase 'the cultured words, / and young bodies' is wrapped lovingly both in the sentimentality of the message in the music and in a cloak of high literary technique (these lines are in Spanish alexandrines, full of anaphora, with the ellipsis marks much loved of the *modernista* poets of the *fin-de-siècle*). It is the dandy's cloak of equivocation: beneath the high art and in this oh-so-coded city of Verona is a statement of radical difference. Unlike many others engaged on the traditional high-minded quest for Time Past or for the perfect realm beyond, Villena distils his 'drop of *pure Time*: of Time without time' (p.313) from glorious banalities and gay commonplaces while still also valuing them for the ideals they signify. He loves mixing kitsch and metaphysics. In other remembered adventures in this poem he values 'the boys [on the beach] walking and playing and going up and down / and the yankee woman with the tortoiseshell glasses with heart-shaped frames' (p.313); and there are conversations with sexy French boys making rum cocktails while the snow falls outside,

> conversaciones – alcohol por medio –
> en que la más sutil metafísica de amor
> carece de importancia y es a la par terrible.
> ¿Se desnudaron? ¿Hablaron de sus vidas?
>
> (p.314)

conversations – with alcohol around – / in which the subtlest metaphysics of love/loses all importance and yet is terrible too. / Did they take their clothes off? Did they talk about their lives?

Consciousness of the disruptive and erotically trangressive potential in the landscapes of ruins and classicism is not new to Spanish writing and art. Lorca's play *El público (The Public)* has an outrageous second act where two figures, one dressed in bells, the other in vine-leaves, act out a verbal and choreographed S/M routine against the backdrop of Roman ruins which are used, it is clearly implied, for casual sex and from which emerges an Emperor, in search of his former male lover (one of the dancing actors) and guarded by a comical hyper-macho Centurion.[6] In 'San Rafael,

6. On this scene see Paul Julian Smith, *The Body Hispanic: Gender and Sexuality in Spanish and Spanish American Literature*, Oxford, 1989, pp.132–5: '[the scene] unfolds in the desecrated remains of the cultural monument, the "theatre" of Nietzsche's decadent Europe. Lorca's intermittent and parodic references to Antiquity [...] deny us the chance to recognize ourselves in his characters and undermine our sense of the reality of history [...] [The Figures'] perpetual changes preclude any illusion of psychic continuity' (p.133).

Córdoba' from the *Romancero gitano* (*Gypsy Ballads*) the archaeology of Córdoba – gleaming marble columns and a 'naked Roman torso', and a Moorish overlay (the presence of the Mosque, reference to the symbolic crescent moon and the dual allegiance of Raphael himself to Islam and Christianity) – forms a complicated counterpoint to homoerotic play by naked boys in the water of the Guadalquivir.[7] Villena himself makes representation of the male body in Lorca a central concern in an article on these famous poems and he concerns himself specifically with Lorca's 'desiring the masculine' and 'describing male desire'.[8] The presiding angel of this ballad is read by Villena as a metaphor of union of the sacred and profane (like San Miguel and San Gabriel in two other ballads), as the most sensual of Lorca's angels and as the representative both of the 'obviously phallic' fish the boys are teasing in the poem and of the iconic boys and their 'masculine charms' ('Sensibilidad homoérotica', p.28).

The artist Gregorio Prieto – who, as Sahuquillo discreetly puts it, 'knew Lorca well and lived for some time with Cernuda' (*Cultura homosexual*, p.132) – takes us even further into the transgressively significant landscapes of ruins to link Mediterranean with gay cultures.[9] In *Lorca y su mundo angélico* (*Lorca and his Angelic World*, 1972), Prieto (again according to Sahuquillo) 'makes himself pretty clearly understood, perhaps too much so, when one thinks that Spain was still living under the dictatorship' when rhapsodically he characterises Lorca's work as '"archangelic"', both '"male and female"' (Sahuquillo, *Cultura homosexual*, p.131). Indeed, Prieto declares straight out that 'Federico es *in*. Federico es *camp*. Federico es pop' (*Mundo angélico*, p.173). The illustrations themselves are clearer still, with sailors, a half-naked male figure with drawn-on wings (p.173) and, as Sahuquillo might have gone on to point out, a dominant aesthetic of camp and kitsch in the flightiness of the

7. Federico García Lorca, *Obras completas*, 3 vols, Madrid, 1987, vol. 1, pp.412–13.
8. 'La sensibilidad homoerótica en el *Romancero gitano*', *Campus* (University of Granada), no. 27 (December 1986), pp.27–30. 'En efecto, desear lo masculino, describir el deseo masculino, o pintar esa masculinidad en su violencia o su gracia es siempre el modo que adopta en *Romancero gitano* la exaltación de la sexualidad – sin objetivos – que es su tema' (p.27). See also Paul Binding, *Lorca: The Gay Imagination*, London, 1984, pp.57–68.
9. Prieto was made a member of the Real Academia de Bellas Artes de San Fernando (Madrid) in 1990, and the same year saw the inauguration of the Museo Gregorio Prieto in his native Valdepeñas (Castilla-La Mancha). He died on 14 November 1992.

collage and the feyness of the colouring throughout the book.
Prieto's *Paintings and Drawings*[10] (which include a glamorous
portrait of Lorca, giving him the air of a Montgomery Clift)[11]
constantly interweave classical and homoerotic motifs. Male
couples kiss as two women look on – either curious, or redundant
– from the balcony of a brothel in 'The Lupanar in Pompeii'; 'Boy
Reading' and 'The River' are very 'Greek' in tone; 'Narcissus' is a
full-lipped youth embracing erotically another naked figure's
lower legs (plates 5, 31, 40 and 45). The large-scale painting
'Taormina' (plate 9) is an icon of the whole tradition, bringing
homoerotic counter-culture and Mediterranean orthodox culture
into a transgressive embrace: it has sailors cruising each other and
hugging in the stylised ruins.

Villena's poem 'Placer de ruinas' ('The Pleasure of Ruins') in *As
To A Foreign Place* (*Lugar extraño*, pp.87–8) reflects on an anthology
of Golden Age poems on ruins prepared by the Hispanist Stanko
Vranich (who is not in any way implicated in Villena's
interpretations).[12] It begins (in an archaising tone maintained
throughout)

> Troya, Roma, Itálica o Cartago . . .
> Es muy bello, Vranich, perorar de ruinas
> y mecerse entre sus mil significados.
>
> (p.87)

> Rome, Troy, Italica or Carthage . . . / It is most pleasant, Vranich, to
> muse upon the ruins / and be carried on the current of their thousand
> meanings.

But the particular meanings chosen here, guided by a tradition
other than the straight classical, follow the lines of transgressive
desire: the ruins in this poem are human ruins, boys who have lost
their perfect beauty as they have aged but who have gained a new,
perverse and piquant edge (and may be slept with again, hence the
special 'pleasures of ruins'). Boys who generate a flawed but
powerfully sexy attraction: 'guardan asimismo un resto de la
esencia, / más concentrada y fuerte, excitante por ello y

10. Gregorio Prieto, *Paintings and Drawings*, London, 1947.
11. *Paintings And Drawings*, plate 11. Also reproduced, poorly, in Lorca, *Obras*, vol. 3,
12. Stanko B. Vranich (ed.), *Los cantores de las ruinas en el Siglo de Oro*, Ferrol, 1981.

empalmera' (p.88: 'they still have lingering none the less the remains of their essence, / which being stronger and now concentrated excites and makes desire stand proud'). An attraction which leads away from bars and discos and away from the cruelties of ageing towards the allegorical landscapes of transgression and the complexities of the aesthetics of decline.

The South, the South: Affiliations

An archetypal space for the interchange, intersection and evasion of cultures is the South (even from the Spanish perspective). In imagination Villena follows the likes of Beckford, Byron, Baron Corvo, Douglas, Firbank, Keats, Baudelaire, Rimbaud and Wilde (all of whom he has written about as a critic);[13] in the preface to *To Flee from Winter* the South is a site of encounter with 'the prematurely interrupted tradition of Greco-Latin paganism [...] and Hellenism, which brings with it the Orient, and the best aspect of Islam' (*Poesía*, p.201),[14] and it is not only a place of grand aspirations and a site for replotting culture but, like classical ruins, a familiar homosexual topos.

Like Lorca, Villena undertakes a quest for aesthetic origins in aspects of Islam. 'Ibn Arabi busca la rosa en el laberinto' ('Ibn Arabi Looks For The Rose In The Labyrinth') in *Sublime Solarium* (*Poesía*, pp.79–80) enthusiastically and neo-surrealistically bonds together naked bodies, the heady perfume of flowers, the dark foam of the sea, sand, panthers, tigers, gold, orgasm and a vague orientalism:

> lentas mitologías de dioses o zalemas en faz de terciopelo, un segundo en las playas del estío, el mar como tus ojos, recuerdos de sirenas en noches de abalorios o de espumas de ónix y después, cimitarra de luz que se pierde en la tarde, después de los magnolios viene siempre el olvido . . . (p.80)

> slow mythologies of gods or sweeping Eastern courtesies of velvet aspect, a single second on the beaches of summer, the sea like your eyes, memories of sirens on nights made of beads of glass or onyx foam and then, a scimitar of light which fades into the evening, for always after walking through magnolias comes oblivion . . .

13. See Introduction, note 6 above Robert Aldrich, *The Seduction of the Mediterranean: Writing, Art and Homosexual Fantasy* (London, 1993) is a useful recent compendium.
14. Villena expands on this in 'Cuerpo y placer en el Mediterráneo', *Cuadernos Hispanoamericanos*, no. 468 (June 1989), pp.105–16.

'La noche del poeta árabe' ('An Arab Poet Goes Out By Night'),
'Reinos de Taifas' ('Taifa Kingdoms'), 'Para honrar a Ibn Hazm de
Córdoba' ('In Honour of Ibn Hazm of Córdoba') and 'Para honrar
a Ibn Quzman, zejelero' ('In Honour of Ibn Quzman, Performer of
Zejels') in *Hymnica* (pp.173–4, 176–7, 180–1 and 183–4) all reconstruct the associational link of Islam with sex, male beauty, wine
and, in the last instance, music.

In 'Al-Andalus' from *To Flee From Winter* (pp.208–9), which
portrays a tea-dance in the old homosexual style, music serves to
link these strands to Villena's personal theme of escape from
Madrid or Spain, while adding the (much needed) piquancy of an
oblique and ironic glance at both the pseudo-Islamicising tradition
itself and the gloriously seamy, absurder side of camp homosexual
lifestyles still surviving from a previous age:

¿Quién está junto al músico?
Bajo la araña de cristal, suenan
sones antiguos, y sus ojos negros
contemplan el moverse del teclado.
Beben alrededor viejos de afeites,
y un mimo malo imita a una cantante
anciana. ¡Pero los ojos . . .!
es la pura belleza con oriente.

(p.208)

But who is that there next to the pianist? / Beneath the crystal
chandelier sounds / from the past ring out, and his dark eyes /
contemplate the movement on the keys. / Older men with just a little
make-up drink around them / and a bad drag artiste impersonates a
singer / from long ago. But those eyes . . .! / Pure beauty with a touch
of the orient.

The boy's presence is a double redemption here. The drag act
scenario is more than just its tedious self and can gesture to a better
world; secondly, the boy's beauty allows the gossipy-camp narrator
to slip over from the mundanity of the immediate environs and,
as it were, better himself by association with Luis Antonio de
Villena's more sophisticated world of ideal forms. Almost
comically, too, the reverse process is set in motion and Villena's high
aspirations are given this nice self-conscious twist: instead of the
usual fetishisation of the boy's hair, chest, lips, waist, there is the
surprising (though apt) concentration on his 'his lovely femurs
when he walks' and 'a nice taut iliac crest / enmeshed – look! – with

that soft flesh' (p.208). The excessive attention to anatomy, which obliquely represents both the rapacious gazes of the older queens in the bar and the meticulousness of some imagined oriental dancing master, energises and subverts the idealisation of the boy's beauty. The South is all but forgotten until the final short third part of the poem, which, with an elliptical allusion to the old theme of love as war, also returns to traditional discourses of love:

> ¿Final? ¿Cambios? ¿Batallas?
> A mí me gusta este reino.
> ¿Dónde vivir si no? ¿Africa?
> ¿En Africa? . . .

(p.209)

> The end of the story? Changes? Battles? / I like this realm. / Where to live if not here? Africa?
> In Africa . . .?

And the structure rehearses the promising blankness which – Eurocentrically – the South, the desert, is deemed to be (an attitude developed at length in the representation of the dissident Álvaro in *Beyond The World*).

Another question 'Where?' is put in 'Seguro bálsamo contra la tristeza' ('A Sure and Certain Balm for Sadness') in *To Flee from Winter* (p.262). At first it seems here that a fairly comprehensive answer is offered, and it is what in 'Viento del sur' ('South Wind') (pp.248-9) the Baron von Gloeden is said to have found: 'ancient passions (amid red anemones)' (p.248). In the end, however, there is no knowing whether to settle on literary images or on sex alone, whether to take the quest in seriousness or in wry half-jest:

> ¿Hacia dónde el sur? [...]
> ¿Con qué hay que romper para llegar allá? ¿Por qué está siempre lejos su verano de frutos licorosos [...]?
> ¿Dónde esa
> música astral de jazmines y lenguas; sus cuerpos
> entre el agua y el vapor con olor de lentisco y alheña?
> ¿Qué es el Sur? ¿Dónde está el eterno verano
> de los griegos? ¿O el *Libro de la Flor* de Ibn Dawud? [...]
> ¿Dónde el inmenso sur, el olor dulce del brotar seminal;
> el glabro abdomen terso para morir de amor, allí?
> ¿Dónde ese sur buscado noche a noche para ser feliz?

Where to look for the south? [...] / [...] / What must be left behind to get there? Why are the liquor-brimming / fruits of its summer distant always [...]? / [...] / Where is / that astral harmony in tongues and jasmine; their bodies / in the water, smelling of mastic and of henna? / What is the South? Where is the eternal summer / of the Greeks? / Or Ibn Dawud's *The Book of the Flower*? / [...] / Where the expansive south, the sweet smell of outpouring seed; / the taut, smooth-skinned abdomen to let us die for love, there and then? / Where is the south where night by night we seek happiness?

There is a pull towards the physical act of sex here, away from those idealistic night-time searches for impossible love, away from just books at bedtime, and away, apparently, from (European) culture; it disrupts and invalidates the whole sequence of questions, including the most important rhetorical and submerged question, 'is it not romantically delightful, symbolically essential not in fact to know?'. This rebellious discourse is even stronger in 'Al sur en una pequeña ciudad provinciana' ('In the South in a Small Provincial Town') (pp.265–6) where the South becomes a composite place, a mix of inland and Mediterranean Andalusia:

Y me imagino paseando aquellas calles
donde llegará el olor del mar y del campo.
Recorriendo un poco ocioso, aljamas
y juderías, y bebiendo – a la tarde – el vino
caliente de las tabernas. Charlando
de pescado y flores, con vecinos. Ofreciendo
cigarros y guardando para mí las alegrías
más íntimas: La cabeza vista en el Museo,
las páginas del libro leídas por la noche,
mientras el sueño me llega con murmullo
de mar, y arde entre los labios la metáfora. [...]

Hacia el sol y el sur el camino es muy largo.
Hay que despojarse y enriquecerse de muchas cosas.
Pero no tengo miedo.
Sé que me hablarán las gentes
que amo, y que no me faltará un cuerpo joven
en la noche de invierno. Primigenia belleza
que ya admiro: Vello y joyel como un poema
leído en Ibrahim Ibn Sahl, musulmán sevillano.

And I see myself strolling through those streets / which are reached by the smell of the sea and the fields. / Wandering rather leisurely through Moorish / and Jewish quarters, and drinking – at evening-time – the warm wine / in old-fashioned bars. Chatting / about flowers and the price of fish, with neighbours. Passing / cigarettes around and keeping for myself the most private joys: / The bust seen in the museum, / the pages of a book read at night / as sleep comes with the murmur / of the sea, and a metaphor burns between my lips.[...] The road to the sun and the south is very long. / One must cast off so much and enrich oneself with many things. / But I am not afraid. / I know that those I love will speak to me, / and that I shall not lack for a young body / in the winter nights. That original beauty / such as I now admire: soft down and exquisite jewel, as in a verse / by the Moorish poet Ibrahim Ibn Sahl of Seville.

Casting referentially here and there, rather than the blankness of not-civilisation and a retreat from sex and complexity, the poem – perversely enough – finds yet another site of excess and burning sensual lyricism. Neither nights of sex and drugs nor a retreat into Deia-like hippyism, but an exotic position which is specifically taken from an immediate homosexual culture but which eludes it and rewrites it too. The metaphor burning on the lips shows where the movements away from and back into culture intersect, where the ecstasies of the body and the ecstasies of the text can meet.

3

Cultural Transgressions

Literary Affiliations, Cultural Resistances

*V*illena's composite Mediterranean, as discussed in the previous chapter, is inscribed with cultural meanings not only over the wide range explored by the texts we have just been looking at but also, more specifically, within the more proximate cultural context of Spanish poetry after Lorca. In the essay 'Lapitas y centauros' ('Lapiths and centaurs', 1981), writing on Spanish poetry of the 1970s, Villena places himself in line with a wide range of significant transgressive others thus affirming both his difference from mainline Spanish cultural practice and his literary (as well as personal) affiliations.[1] The poets Jaime Gil de Biedma (1929–90), Francisco Brines (b. 1932) and José Manuel Caballero Bonald (b.1928) are admired for the way in which they 'reinstate every forbidden aesthetic – which is rather like saying they reinstate aesthetics itself' ('Lapitas', p.14). Villena sees them, at that time, as having a vital 'will to difference' and having been able to link up with 'the Europeanising tendencies of the Generation of 1927' as well as with 'important traditions of intertextual writing' in the rest of Western Europe and North America which, he says, 'the Spanish post-war period had no use for' (p.14). Auden, Cavafy, Cernuda, Pablo García Baena (b.1923, one of the Córdoba-based 'Cántico group' of poets) and Brines are all involved in reworking and reinterpreting the tradition of classicism in poetry and working towards a synthesis of 'the aesthetic tradition' and 'experience' (p.16).

Brines's engagement with the transgressive aesthetic is of particular interest, not least because of its tentativeness and ambiguity. *Poemas a D.K.* (*Poems to D.K.*, 1986) and *El otoño de las rosas* (*The Autumn of the Roses*, 1986) reveal an engagement with

1. 'Lapitas y centauros: (Algunas consideraciones sobre la nueva poesía española en la última década)', *Quimera*, no. 12 (October 1981), pp.13–20.

homoeroticism which links him closely with Villena. In earlier poems belonging to a less liberal era this engagement is more tacit and Brines uses the Mediterranean journey both to veil and reveal his own going away to 'come out' from the old cultural and sexual experience into the new. In Part II of *Palabras a la oscuridad* (*Words for the Darkness*, 1966) a 'Traveller' leaves his Valencian home to become the 'Stranger' who, following some golden-haired youths, ends up in Italy, where more youths loll about in the ruins, among statues, or bathe and play on the sea-shore, where a local museum displays a fine Saint Sebastian (which gay icon even in Spain in the 1960s would have spoken loud and clear).[2] 'Versos épicos' ('Epic Verses') (Brines, *Poesía*, pp.79–80), with the epigraph 'Virgil en Trápani', has the poet very tentatively frame two youths down on the beach, placing them in the new transgressive context: 'es muy baja mi voz. / Os miro' ('my voice very quiet, / I watch you') he declares and the quietness of the voice denotes the (now obvious) forbidden love (p.80). Remembering the lovers Nisus and Euryalus from the *Aeneid* the speaker projects onto the swimming boys an epic future of exile, love and bitterness which will come of their pact, 'the firm decision' taken in this place (p.80).

Brines's strategy is a gentle if none the less clear homosexual recoding both of the classicism and the emerging *culturalismo* of many of his contemporaries. Cernuda's earlier treatment of the theme of the Mediterranean South is also, as a matter of course, homoeroticised. In the much-read three-part poem 'Resaca en Sansueña' ('Ebb Tide in Sansueña') in *Las nubes* (*The Clouds*, 1940)[3] a gay and classicised Eden is imagined:

El aroma del mar vasto y denso suspende
Los mortales dormidos bajo un clásico encanto,
Y modela los cuerpos con fuertes líneas puras,
Y en las venas infiltra las pasiones antiguas.

Con la gracia inocente de esbeltos animales
Se mueven en el aire estos hombres sonoros,
Bellos como la luna, cadenciosos de miembros,
Elásticos, callados, que ennoblecen la fuerza.

2. Francisco Brines, *Poesía 1960–1981*, Madrid, 1984, pp.73–7.
3. In Luis Cernuda, *Poesía completa*, ed. Derek Harris and Luis Maristany, Barcelona, 1974, pp.230–5. Sansueña is an imaginary place, generally understood to be an amalgam of archetypal southern coastal town and Spain itself.

Las mentiras solemnes no devoran sus vidas
Como en el triste infierno de las ciudades grises.
(Cernuda, *Poesía completa*, pp.230–1)

The aroma of the widespread density of sea suspends / in a classical
enchantment the lives of these sleeping mortals, / and models their
bodies in strong, pure lines, / and infiltrates ancient passions in their
veins.
With the innocent grace of lithe, lean animals / these sweet-sounding
men move on the breeze, / as lovely as the moon, their limbs
harmonious in motion / quiet, athletic, ennobling their strength.
Their lives are not devoured by solemn lies / as in the sad inferno of
the grey, drab city.

In *Corsairs in Yellow Gloves* Villena reads these lines, which at a
superficial reading seem so gently full of a rather orthodox
nostalgia, as being alive with the spirit of rebellion, as a defiant act
of recuperation and reconstruction. The male bodies here are 'the
(magnificent) remains of what is to be found in life here and now
of that lost Eden', moments of plenitude which are to be found
inscribed 'in the beauty of the adolescent body [...] in the poetic text
which bridges those tremendous distances [between reality and
desire]' (*Corsarios*, p.146). The writing of this body of desire is
Cernuda's key act of rebellion: 'as with the dandy, [Cernuda's] real
world is his performance, his stage, that is to say his art' (p.146).
So visions of a Mediterranean and homoerotic Eden are part of the
enlivening, precise, and quite un-deluded art of the rebel and
dandy. Classical harmony is invoked not in nostalgia for discipline,
purity, or access to the spiritual: Villena reads 'harmony' quite
otherwise since 'the rebel is such because he aspires to a certain
harmony, and in this harmony he cultivates his self [...] knowing
it, self-consciously, to be different, triumphant in spite of disaster'
(p.147). Villena goes on to say that he is himself engaged on the
problematic quest for a harmony which is at the same time a
dissenting voice. In *The Journey to Byzantium* and *Hymnica* he is
writing what he calls a 'personal and sensualist version' through
a 'poetry of experience' of the classical (especially Hellenistic) and
Symbolist aesthetic traditions (p.147). When he talks of his 'poetry
of experience' it is vital to remember that it is a lived homoerotic
experience as well as elaborate aesthetic experience which is being
referred to, an ethics based on being (albeit mostly gladly and
with no declared hardship) at the margins of established society.

It is the experience of living in and through a coherent counter-culture predicated on outlawed desire and behaviour. However, his affiliations, the insistence on particular forms of resistance and the very coherence of Villena's strategy all encourage his inclusion in established cultural categories and a normalisation of his rebellion.

In a rare politicised discussion of homosexuality in the cultural context of the Spanish late 1970s A. S. Rey notes, from a New Marxist viewpoint, that bourgeois liberal values are as likely in Spain as anywhere else in capitalist Europe to construct the mythical red herring of the 'sensitive artist type' and through this construction 'determine a specific sensibility [...] a "special sensitivity"' ('una "gran sensibilidad"').[4] Rey identifies as a particular risk the targeting in such readings of a kind of 'taste which inclines very much towards the baroque, the decorative, for farce and playfulness' (p.43). The identification of an 'aesthetics of "queens"' ('la estética de las "locas"') means that 'everything can be reduced down to the explanation that the homosexual artist is doing none other than sublimating his libido' (p.43). And worse:

> What can be isolated, catalogued, and labelled loses its rebarbative character. This way the good bourgeois may go to a play by Lorca, see films like *A Man Called 'Autumn Flower'* or read Cavafy with no danger, without having to challenge themselves in any way, since this is 'queer' stuff, crazy people's stuff, for people who don't belong. (p.43)[5]

The immediate cultural context of homoerotic writing with which Villena is engaging is indeed full of invitations to read a 'sensibility' into the texts. Brines in particular is one whose texts for part of the time swing close to susceptibility to the good 'bourgeois' reading feared by Rey. The austerity and the dialogue with honoured literary traditions in his poems, as well as their frequently melancholy tone, all invite a normalising reading, an acceptance into the fold.[6] There are however also important

4. A.S. Rey, 'La estética gay', in the special feature 'Dossier Homosexualidad', *Ozono*, no. 39 (December 1978), pp.42–3, p.43.
5. *Un hombre llamado 'Flor de Otoño'* (*A Man Called 'Autumn Flower'*, 1977), directed by Pedro Olea, director of *The Fencing Master* (on release in Britain June 1993) and one of the principal figures in the Spanish Cinema of the Transition to Democracy.
6. On this aspect of Brines, see Chris Perriam, 'The Body in the Shadows: Transgressive voices in the poetry of Francisco Brines', *Journal of Hispanic Research*, vol. 2 (1993–4), pp.369–83.

moments where a textual dissidence makes orthodox readings problematic. Brines, like Villena, comes back constantly to the specificity of sex: the body, the act of 'love', interposes to block the idealising retreat into the past of tradition or the future or the other of a transcendent reality. By 1980, Brines is able to recognise 'just how much of a moral disruptive homoeroticism is for many of the younger generation' and see 'its attraction as a sign of freedom'.[7] Homosexuality, he observes, 'has always been the most immovable of tabus [...] [Cernuda and Cavafy] not only defended homosexuality but went as far as to exalt it [...] To take up this position represented a frontal attack on the very core of conventional morality' (Burdiel, *Brines*, pp.22–3).

In their different ways of centring on the 'moral disruptive' of the body of homoeroticism Brines and, more so, Villena coincide with the 'transgressive aesthetic' of Wilde as read by Dollimore (*Sexual Dissidence*) and are perverting the dominant cultural order. Smith summarises one stage of Dollimore's argument in this way: 'The "proximate" nature of deviance (of homosexuality), its very closeness to the heterosexuality that seeks to exclude it, enables it to "track back" in a "transgressive reinscription" as an anti-essentialist agency freed from the humanist illusions of autonomous selfhood' (Smith, *Laws*, p.11). Brines in particular risks an anti-transgressive (yet perverse) dynamic whereby homoerotic dissidence tracks away to become safely readable and labelled, as Rey says, as '"queer" stuff' precisely because of its complicity with 'illusions of autonomous selfhood'. There are texts by both writers which risk the unchallenging readings identified by Rey, which put them away in the realm of the Other, making them conform to the 'sensitive artist type', readings which want to interpret dissident adventures in Experience and Art as simply manifestations of the time-honoured quest for a true or truer self through Love and through imaginative projection. However, there are also the texts which are structured around and construct that 'moral disruptive' of Brines's, which look to 'illustrious forms' and 'bodies beautiful and bought', as Villena puts it in 'Excellent Plans for the Future'. Like Dollimore's trangressive (pre-Reading Gaol) Wilde, these texts privilege form, the surface, cultural and sexual difference.

Resisting the drift towards idealism, essence, metaphysics, deep

7. Isabel Burdiel, *Francisco Brines*, Cuadernos de Cultura Quervo, Valencia, 1980, p.23.

and easy answers, Villena insists on the relations between textuality and sexuality and on a trangressive practice of these relations, particularly in *The Journey to Byzantium*. Its prefatory text, 'Inicial', ends with the declaration that 'art is effort, ecstasy, signs on the air, pleasure, reality and artifice' (*Poesía*, p.116). The poems suggest that art is a relating of textual conventions and controls to the sudden, apparently arbitrary movements of desire, a spiralling around and in and out of the apparently different areas of body and culture until they are conjured into the same.

Transfigurations

In 'Piscina' (p.127: 'Swimming Pool'), written in 1973, the body of a sexy young swimmer is framed in a near-sonnet (one of several such in the book) which lightly and playfully disobeys the metrical and structural conventions it half bows to. Just as the bars and streets of the city are so often transfigured by the minor gods of Villena's myths of desire, so here a common urban afternoon scene is made extraordinary as a boy dives to the water:

> y el desnudo se goza un instante en el aire,
> para astillar después en vibraciones verdes
> el oro y el azul y la espuma que canta.

and the naked figure revels in itself for an instant in the air, / to splinter then into vibrating greens / the gold and the blue and the singing flurried water.

The swimmer leaves himself behind at this epiphany and abandons the present to become a boy-nymph whose movements become the centre-point of a highly sensual conceit of baroque flavour which allows the reader to delight in a series of exquisite contradictions. Villena manages a combination of classical and pastoral-piscatorial images with elements taken from popular homoerotic or commercialised erotica. The literary form and resonance tenses against the looseness of the subject matter which is at no more than one remove from soft-porn material:

> Desciendes un momento. Y riela en los visos
> del cristal transparente el fuego que galopa
> entre las ramas verdes, y es túnica
> de seda que amorosa recoge la selva de tu cuerpo [...]
> te complaces en verte en grutas submarinas.

> For a moment you descend. And in the glinting / of transparent crystal
> the fire shimmers / as it gallops through the green branches above,
> and is a silken / tunic fondly wrapping the wild forest of your body
> / [...] / you delight to see yourself in caves beneath the sea.

As in a story out of Ovid, with the sun-god in his chariot presiding, the boy shifts from element to element, enchanting the natural world about him; he shifts from classical to decadent as that tunic takes hold and begins to enchant in a less decorous and harmonious way. The intellectual, readerly pleasures of these structures of wit and rhythm and the allusions are strong: Spanish readers in particular would be reminded of the style of the seventeenth-century poet Góngora who is also honoured in two outrageous, baroque pastiches, 'Somnium Divos' and 'Alegórica pintura' ('Allegorical Painting') in *Death Alone* (*Poesía*, pp.334 and 336), and in a portrait poem, 'Joven Góngora' ('Young Góngora') in *As To A Foreign Place* (*Lugar extraño*, pp.89–90). Such literary pleasures, though, are given an unexpected counterpoint in the joyous crudeness of sudden sexual desire manifest in the speaker and expected to be registered vicariously by the reader (who might recode it through his own gym-and-pool-going experiences, through his sightings of advertisements for jeans or swimwear, or just through Hockney). The boy emerges from the pool as the poet addresses him and in doing so draws the reader closer into complicity and voyeurism:

> Y al regresar al sol, nos miras en la orilla
> mientras toda codicias sexuales, el agua
> deseosa,
> se goza solitaria en tu cintura.

> And returning to the sunlight then you look across at us there on the
> edge / while the water, made of sexual longings, plays / desirous and
> alone about your waist.

Around these lines forms another homosexual-cultural association. With the green branches, the metamorphic play, the erotic water and the detail of the 'waist' perhaps comes another Andalusian voice to join Góngora's, that of Lorca, of whom all these features might be said to be a trademark (and, indeed, appear forcefully in the ballad 'San Rafael, Córdoba' discussed briefly in Chapter Two). However, the boy has emerged not just from the water but from out of the world of Literature into the world of erotic experience, only to entice Literature back down into the gloriously superficial depths of his pools of pleasure where the banalities of a metropolitan swimming-pool, the thrills of voyeurism and image consumerism, literary reference and metaphorical pyrotechnics are all one.

A lively culture-clash which makes excess triumphant, socially and culturally vitalising, is constructed more elaborately in 'Atis-Adonis' in *Death Alone* (*Poesía*, p.342). Around the image of the male body the play of artifice and real desire brings on an exhilarating moment of ecstatic loss of control:

> Para guiarme fuera de la melancolía del tiempo
> y del espacio [...]
> Para que dances y otorgues y sucumbas y te multipliques,
> hazme como tú sumiéndome en tu lumbre
> – sol, dureza, miel, vara de nardos, floración de azúcar –
> condúceme
> al cubil donde tu cuerpo fulja.
> Llévame para que sea, como tú, un inmortal
> que muere, y vivamos sucesivos en quienes gozan su
> lucha fingida y el sexo de los sueños, y birlan
> un alcohol en el supermercado, y gritan de placer cuando
> se miran. Condúceme: Muerto como tú y vivo como tú
> para gustar el solo nombre de la Vida. (La que Rilke
> intuyó, mas no vivió; la que George parodió sumiso.)
> Y ahora abre tu camisa, sonríe como anoche, arrodíllate
> acaso, y ofrece el nítido pecho al sabio puñal de un mito.
> Tú, Puma, Felino, Gato, Príncipe leopardo altivo . . .

> To guide me away from the melancholia of time / and space [...] / so that you may dance, succumb, submit and multiply, / make me like you, immerse me in your brightness / – sun and firmness, honey, rod of nard and sugar florescence – / lead me to the lair where your body will blaze. / Take me to where like you I'll be one of the immortals / who dies, and let us live on in those who follow us, who pleasure themselves / in wrestling games and the sex of their dreams, and pinch / alcohol from supermarket shelves and yelp with joy when / they look at one another. Lead me on: I'll die like you and live like you / to savour the single name of Life. (Which Rilke / once intuited but never had. Which Stefan George just parodied in abjection.) / And pull open your shirt now, smile like you did last night, kneel down / perhaps, and offer up your perfect chest to the dagger thrust of myth. / You, my Puma, my Cat, my Feline, my High Leopard Prince . . .

'Atis-Adonis' (as the title implies) is all about metamorphosis. It is subversive of cultural and textual norms in a number of illuminating and contradictory ways. Strongly traditional – old-fashioned, indeed – is the poem's exploitation of accumulation and repetition (what in another age, the age it is partly subverting, would have been called *gradatio* and *anaphora*). The whole build-up to a moment of revelation at the end of the poem makes the poem sound traditional, even moral in import, like a Spanish Golden-Age text of *desengaño* (where the reader, the spectator, or the addressee of a sonnet, typically, will be taken by the speaker or actor through a narrative or rhetorical process of demystification, or dis-illusionment, to reveal the vanity of outward things). In the section omitted in my quotation the poem has been high in tone with allusions to mystic and mythical discourses. The boy is angelic guide, Adonis the huntsman, Cupid, attendant of Bacchus, Argonaut. But myth and ageless epic quest combine with the age of the Vespino, Arcadia mixes with modern Mediterranean street-life, and a suggestion of the Homeric is ousted by a hint of Matt Dillon as the desire is expressed 'to sail with you, an Arcadian / explorer, one of the Roman gang on the motorbikes of night' ('el hermano de razzia en la moto nocturna'). The fantasies ride, and Atis-Adonis is surprisingly transformed. When he is brought down to earth after that climactic and excessive line with sun at one end and sugar at the other (a considerable and a risky lyrical leap) the boy-god might still be a soaring angel but celestial light is transmuted into the more sensual glow of a body in a lair which – given the context – might be a dim-lit bedroom or back-room anywhere in modern Madrid. The dancing which might have been the boy-god's response to a celestial music shades into something more closely associated, as the contexts shift, with disco-dancing. Balsam becomes more the sensually obvious 'honey', the delicate garland is changed for the blatant nard (much favoured by Lorca in his more sensual lines). These shifts from the abstract and the excited 'firmness' give a salient sense of what is really being asked for in this invocation. In an overturning of procreation-oriented myths and religions, the outcome of the heavenly boy's contact with an earthly being in an earthy context and his becoming, like Christ-Atis-Adonis, 'an immortal / who dies' is a spawning (a 'multiplication') of attractively street-wise and libidinous youths, a kind of mildly William Burroughs brotherhood. The high tragedy of the death of a god mingles with the baser, sexual significance which is coaxed out of the word 'dies' by the yelps of pleasure; there is the sudden glorious descent into the coarse and period-specific detail of the drink stolen from the supermarket which eclipses the previous balsam: these are postmodern metamorphoses, sharp with a sense of the mutability of schemes of values. Here the lesson, going against the traditional grain, is that not only are the outward things the true source of revelation, but that the inward things are so bound up in them that of themselves they lack all value. For the duration of those 'yelps of pleasure', this brotherhood and the Adonis who presides over and fathers them, are eternal life, the answer to a prayer. Their raw pleasure and their eye-contact inflect the lines that follow; the figures of high culture, and their failure, are bracketed off, with Rilke particularly losing out since the thirteen syllables which in the Spanish line precede the parenthesis containing his name have a powerful rhythmic pattern which is already strongly rounded off, and the continuation of the pattern after full stop and parenthesis has an illustratively pathetic redundancy.

The last lines of the poem operate another shift. Expected as the conclusion of the prayer to the boy-god to whom the poet has been in thrall, it enters in on a new scenario where the boy is sex-slave to the poet-master. The transcendental language has now quite disappeared and the desire to escape time and place have been forcibly replaced by other desires, in the here and now. Invocations cast prospectively into an unreal realm are now direct commands. Quite disrupted is the earlier expectation of a traditional revelation of wisdom at the poem's end as the rhetorical climax arrives in the words beginning 'And now open up . . .'. The stylistically shameless, pulsing endearments of the final line, in what is now a scene of ritualized sex, elevate Atis-Adonis to a new position, at the pinnacle of a moment's pleasure when desire overrides restraints and everything is at the surface of the skin. The youth who is to submit to the 'knowing dagger-thrust of myth' becomes not only an object of desire but penetrated through with desires constructed in myths and literature – not a few of which are alluded to in this poem.[8] It is typical of homosexual cultural style that here so many high ideas are focused in the form of the receptive youth unbuttoning his shirt, that such traditional textual strategies allow such unorthodox associations, that ordinary notions of good taste and bad taste cannot be brought to this text. It becomes enjoyably impossible to tell whether the sex in the air is heavenly or whether

8. For a reading of the symbol of the dagger which avoids the usual academic coyness, see Sahuquillo, *Cultura homosexual*, pp.135–40.

the things not of this world are what are really desired, whether Villena's wish is to be outside time or in that room, whether better the veil half-seen through or the shirt unbuttoned.

'Una contradanza' ('A Contra-dance') in *As To A Foreign Place* (*Lugar extraño*, pp.23–5) begins by proposing a classicising and idealist reading of the body in the tradition shared by Francisco Brines. The body here is 'permanent', 'full' and 'rounded to the mouth' but simultaneously it is 'unreachable perfume' and the 'temptation of the realm beyond' (p.23). The poem, traditionally now for Villena, calls on renaissance art and Neoplatonism (the boy's flesh is 'like marble' and he signifies perfect beauty: p.23) and after the late renaissance manner makes the object of desire the emblem of transience. As the steps of the contra-dance become more intricate though, this established convention is subverted:

Noche del cuerpo, sombra caliente que sin decirlo
habla, murmurio de eternidad
que tocas con los dedos, y escapa vuelto flor,
como el más raudo río, en tanto ardor
– noche del cuerpo, violencia de la carne –
en tanta pasión y caudal,
fuga de primavera . . .
¡Cuánta fue la delicia! Y aún está ahí,
y aún apetece y turba, y trastorna los sentidos
y hace música y noche, aún, tan perfecto,
tan eterno y huyente, hermoso cuerpo en juventud,
gloria nocturna, perfume, vaho, evanescente ardencia . . .

(p.23)

Dark night of the body, warm shadow which saying nothing, / speaks: the murmur of eternity / which you touch with your fingers and it escapes transformed into a flower / like the fullest roaring river, in fervour / – dark night of the body, violence of the flesh – in such torrent and passion, it is the fugue of springtime . . . / Such ecstasy it was! And it is yet there, / and still incites, perturbs, and disarrays the senses / and makes music and night, still so perfect, / so eternal and fleeting, a handsome youthful body, / nocturnal glory, perfume, vapour, brief ardency . . .

The ecstasy, as well as sexual, is that of Spanish *poesía pura* (a particularly metaphysical modernism), the line '¡Cuánta fue la delicia! Y aún está ahí' ('Such ecstasy it was! And it is yet there') strongly echoing Jorge Guillén's *Cántico*, and this is consonant with the classicising discourse. It displays a temptation towards the metaphysical. But as we have just heard, the Romantic principle of perturbation and the pull towards the sensual disrupt this control, ushering in, at the end of this first part, or movement, some liberatingly excessive writing and, that favourite indulgence of the followers of *fin-de-siècle modernismo*, the (exceedingly) suggestive dying fall on a climactic ellipsis, 'gloria nocturna, perfume, vaho, evanescente ardencia . . .' ('nocturnal glory, perfume, exhalation, brief ardency. . .': 'ardencia' is a neologism much favoured by Villena). Pulling even more strongly away from harmony and control, though paradoxically also abandoning physicality, are the gestures towards the non-verbal; not just the emphasis on touch, but the not-saying, the murmur and the music. These, instead of going back towards the metaphysical and writing the poem into the modernist tradition of the quest for 'the music of silence', lead to a further abandonment, in the second part of the text (or dance), this time a partial abandonment of the idealising vision of sex. In a later sex act, when the perfection of the boy's beauty has faded but the friendship has matured, the controlled visions of classicism are demystified and movingly replaced with a much closer knowledge of the body's contradictions and meanings:

> Ahí se abre un camino
> donde el sentimiento habrá de prescindir,
> en el vivir, de imágenes concretas . . .
> Un largo sendero presentido hacia adelante.
> Y acariciando sus labios,
> y gozando la mano en su cintura
> ahora levemente imperfecta,
> perdido lo que fuera rigor del mármol,
> humilde, deberías postrarte
> y suplicando decir:
> Me sentí al borde del precipicio,
> y apenas he iniciado el ascenso.
> Me embriagué y di forma a la idea.
> En delirio, juzgué cúspide lo que era simbólico
> favor del ángel, agua para el sediento . . .
> La absoluta divinidad nos destruiría,
> y es necesario, pues, irse cada uno destruyendo,
> trascender las metáforas,
> y caminar en la pasión a ciegas,
> sabiendo que lo visible
> es tan solo el arduo amanecer,
> el alba carmesí de la aventura.

(p.24)

This way lies a road / where feeling, in experience, / will have to do without all concrete images . . . / A pathway stretching forwards, long-imagined. / And caressing his lips, / and your hand taking pleasure at his waist, / with its slight imperfection, / the previous rigour of marble now lost, / you should lay yourself before him in humility / and begging say: / I was, I felt, at the edge of the abyss, / and I have scarcely begun the climb. / I became intoxicated, I gave form to the idea. / In delirium I took to be the highest point / what was only the angel's symbolic favour, water for the thirsty, . . . / Absolute divinity would destroy us, / and so we must each one destroy / transcend the metaphors, / and walk blind in passion, / knowing that the visible / is no more than the harsh breaking light, / adventure's carmine dawn.

So this is not a traditional dying to the body, rather a dying to the idealisations of the body; it is an attempt to use an excess of concrete image (body, river, flower, fire, mouth, hand . . .) to destroy a superfluity of metaphor, to destroy what it most constructs. Sentiment, experience, and adventure are to take up the crusade of Art and at least one model of depth-identity, the loosely Neoplatonic, is repudiated. We are, however, left with the problem of love: in the first part of the contra-dance, obsession and passion allowed the other – the lover – to be kept at a distance, but when the dance moves on and the object of desire begins to be known and starts to deviate from the control of representational convention, desire begins to move in closer and start all over again the movement of temptation towards 'absolute divinity', essence, ideal, denying the contra-dance its counter-cultural dynamic. The tensions between narrative control and the movements of desire are the concern of the following chapter, in which both the narrating subjects and their objects of desire prove incapable of dispensing with all concrete images and are revealed as being controlled by the very metaphors they need to transcend.

4

Framing Love

Icons and Angels

*A*mour Passion is the story of Arturo, a lecturer in art history, and a younger man, Sixto. It is told in the form of a letter to a friend César who relays it to us and comments on it in a final chapter. Arturo is writing ten years on from the start of the story, ostensibly to clarify what César calls certain 'dark areas' ('puntos oscuros') in his life (*Amor Pasión*, p.7). The tale is also a subtly articulated essay on the distinctions between sexual, sentimental, erotic, romantic, truly felt and fictionalised desires. Arturo is in fact constructing and, within the frame of the letter-within-the-text, deconstructing his own sexuality in his narration, excessively encoding the younger man, making him an icon of desire, all as a response to his own repressed desires. Sixto when first seen is represented as Other, as the 'dark area' Arturo is supposed to be describing and delimiting. As Other drawing fearfully close, he destabilises the narrative by drawing Arturo into a vortex of revelations, reinscribing him increasingly in the 'dark area' he is attempting ostensibly to explain, escape and illuminate.

At the beginning of the story Arturo is walking along Recoletos, in the centre of Madrid, with an older, gay colleague, Diego de Bassano, a specialist in the culture of the Spanish Golden Age:

> Hablábamos de libros, supongo, o de una versión de Calderón que estaba por estrenarse. Sólo de eso. Y mirábamos los paseantes, los árboles, chicos y chicas con bolsas deportivas que volverían de la piscina . . . Y yo empecé a mirar a un punto. Insensiblemente, sin darme cuenta. Miraba a un *punto oscuro* (acertaste, César) y poco a poco (nos habíamos sentado en la terraza de un café) me fui dando cuenta de adónde iba mi mirada. Era un chico lo que, sin saber por qué, estaba mirando. (p.13)

> We were talking about books, I suppose, or a new production of Calderón which was about to have its première. Just things like that.

And we were watching the passers-by, the trees, the boys and girls with sports-bags, on their way back, no doubt, from the pool . . . And I began to fix my gaze on a certain spot. Quite unconsciously, without realising, I was looking into a *dark area* (you were right, César) and bit by bit (we had now sat down at a terrace café) I started to realise where my gaze was being drawn to. Quite unknowingly, I was in fact watching a boy.

Sixto is very beautiful: olive-skinned, with dark eyes, longish black hair, svelte, 'with something of the Arabic about him, and perhaps in the background, very tenuously, a suggestion of Malay or Filipino, and a lot of Italian in him too in the exact harmony of the features' (pp.13-14). Arturo narrates himself as having sunk into a state of unknowing before such beauty, as having moved away from culture. He forgets talk, art, and even, literally, books (when he gets up to go he leaves behind on the table a pile of expensive volumes he and Diego Bassano have just bought). But culture returns: his gaze leads as much into the territory of the aesthetic as into the arena of physical attraction and Sixto is never quite able to escape the initial connection with bookishness and Italy. In the same paragraph where the books are forgotten, books are recalled:

> Por supuesto aquel no era amor, creo que tampoco era sexo (aunque el sexo no esté ausente de ningún deseo) creo que era, ante todo – como si se tratase de un heterodoxo poema modernista – una ambigua figuración mágica, dorada, y llena de luz (oscura luz de su piel) de la Belleza. (p.16)

> This was of course not love; it was not, I think, even sex (even though in any desire sex will never quite be absent). I believe it was above all – as if this were some unconventional *modernista* poem, bright-lit by the dark light of his skin, ambiguous – a magical, golden figuring of Beauty.

The true thrust of Arturo's insistent and intensive enmeshing of the younger man in his literary and artistic experience is to rewrite him for himself, for César, for Villena and for us: not for Sixto or even for his sake. The range of reference in the early stages of Arturo's passion threatens to dismember what integrity of personality Sixto has. He is a pool of bright water (p.15), 'a spring in the midst of a forest, a gentle brook where there are deer and grass grows' (p.21); and of their first sexual encounter Arturo says 'when he was naked beside me, when we kissed, I felt an immense sense of wholeness, like ancient man I felt happy and complete, and felt that beauty, the celebrated roses of all beauty were passing, burning, through my lips' (p.22).

The rose and the pastoral motifs meet up in an association with the Baroque and so with Arturo's professional life. First fairly simply, at the end of the first stage of the affair: 'I told myself it had been a fleeting moment, a flower on a summer's day, the name of the rose that I so liked to explicate when talking about the Baroque . . .' (p.25). Also in a straightforward way, towards the end of the novella, the fading of Sixto's youthful beauty (by now he is twenty-four) is associated with the topos of the rose: 'the petals were falling from the sublime rose, the rose all literature has sung of . . . Garcilaso, Góngora, Rioja . . . So many of my favourite sonnets came to mind' (p.86). In one episode the Baroque – and at the centre of it Sixto – represents the intersection of different codings of beauty, sex, regret and self-delusion which strain to move off in their diverse directions but become confused in Arturo's passionate self-delusion and fixed by his gaze. In this case it is represented in the figure of Medoro, from the story of Angelica and Medoro, as treated by Góngora after Ariosto.[1] It is a year after the first encounter. Sixto has spent some of the intervening time in his home town in the province of Jaén (his family are clearly of the class of migrant workers who in the 1960s had to abandon home for the capital). He has also been working as a waiter in Benidorm (not exactly the roaring Benidorm British readers might readily imagine, but one rather archly refined by Arturo – 'a town by the sea dedicated to mass tourism and to pleasure': p.31). This second stage of the affair is initiated by sex in the guest bedroom in César's flat, which is a multiple compromise: Arturo this time confesses retrospectively to real sexual desire for Sixto, but he is not able to take Sixto home (he is living with his girlfriend Carmen), does not tell César at the time he borrows the keys that he is going there with a boy, and the encounter comes across as a commonplace little bourgeois adultery. The sex is rounded off with post-coital photos of Benidorm and Sixto's recounting his erotic (heterosexual) adventures of the summer.

None of this obviousness, though, prevents Arturo from recoding

---

1. Ariosto's poem is the *Orlando Furioso*, Góngora's is the ballad 'Romance de Angélica y Medoro'. The homoerotic potential in the ballad is visible in Dámaso Alonso's edition of it (Madrid, Ediciones Acies, 1962) which has illustrations by Prieto, including one of Medoro looking more like an illustration to Mary Renault's *The Persian Boy* than to a poem by Góngora (p.47).

the encounter and exalting the presence of a boy who is, after all, just a teenager with an appetite for a lot of sex:

> yo creí que se comportaba con más soltura, por decirlo de algún modo, que tenía menos pudores o más hábito que antes. ¡Y era tanta la hermosura, que ahora creí de nuevo ser el elegido por la pura forma, por tan terrible y alta deidad para favorecerme! Moreno, largo; perfecto . . . ¿Qué era? ¿Modelo de Verrochio? ¿El muchacho que Byron encontró, fascinado, entre los turcos, con grandes zaragüelles blancos y el pecho desnudo? Me enseñó unas fotos del verano en Benidorm. Escenas de bar, risas, luces nocturnas, vasos a medio vaciar . . . [...] Las fotos eran malas, y Sixto estaba en ellas mucho peor que en sí mismo, en aquel momento dulce que yo hubiera apetecido eterno. (pp.31–2)

> I thought he was much more relaxed and confident, if I can put it that way, and had fewer hang-ups or was more practised than before. And such was the beauty of it all that I thought once more that I had been visited by pure form, chosen for favour by some terrible and exalted god. Long-limbed and dark-skinned; perfect . . . What was he? A Verrochio model? The boy whom the fascinated Byron came upon among the Turks, with great white breeches and his chest bared? He showed me photos of the summer in Benidorm. Scenes of bars and lights and laughter, half-finished drinks . . . [...] The photographs were poor, and Sixto looked much worse than he did there in the flesh, in that sweet moment which I would have wished eternal.

Sixto eternalised in pictures clashes with Sixto eternalised in more cerebral and aesthetic images; Sixto as the Italian painter's model clashes with Sixto who has just told Arturo about 'a very fiery Italian woman who at the erotic high-point whispered to him, overcome, *"Più forte, bello; più forte . . ."*'(p.31).

This scene is followed by days of wandering, sleeping in a cheap hotel (Arturo going home at dawn), and acting, for Arturo, 'a little like two bohemians at the turn of the century' (p.33). Any positive associations of such an image – with art, with the age of decadent poetry, with daring – are compromised by a visit to the attic flat of Alberto Urgel, 'who really did live a bohemian life' (p.33). They drink gin, listen to rock, talk about books and films (though Sixto, unsurprisingly, 'scarcely spoke': p.34), but the bohemianism turns out to be an obstacle. Urgel will not leave them alone to have sex (which was the plan) but stays around (the classic smoking, drinking bore) and worse still is clearly much taken with the boy (he later sends a crass and queeny note to Arturo: '"Congratulations! But *what* was *that*?! If you want to give me a present one day, worthy of you if not of me, then introduce me to someone *identical!*'": p.36).

Nevertheless, neither this scene, nor the rather empty days of wandering and creeping home at dawn, nor even the potent banalities surrounding the guest-room sex, can disable Arturo's furious associational reconstructing of Sixto. It is remembering the heavy-drinking Alberto Urgel's fascinated gaze which prompts the elaboration of the multiple image which is fixed in the end on the figure of Medoro:

> Todavía hoy si tengo que representar la imagen mejor del muchacho, su plenitud, me esfuerzo en reconstruir aquellos días. [...] A veces pienso que en aquellos días lo que me ataba tanto a Sixto, incluso me encelaba, porque la palabra es propia, era el arquetipo. El que representase de tan viva y exacta manera un ilustre y antiquísimo arquetipo de belleza. La simetría, la proporción (rectitud de nariz, curva de ojos, grosor, tacto de labios) pero a ese canon perfecto añadiéndole, como raro grano de pimienta, como una especia que si tergiversaba el puro sabor, en realidad lo enriquecía, lo hacía más codiciable, el tono oscuro de la piel, las pestañas tupidas y negras, el aire moresco, que acaso no estimase el mero tratadista de la Grecia dórica, pero sí desde luego [...] los sofistas de Siria, los helenísticos que invocó Cavafis. Me dirás que lo que te estoy contando no tiene tanto que ver con la literatura. Pero todo se mezcla mucho. Y si te he descrito una pasión absolutamente *física* – el hecho de que me empalmase apenas verlo – ¿por qué no contar este otro lado, igualmente real, y que para mí existía y pesaba como una fuerza atávica? Sixto era el canon griego (el que ha perseguido buena parte del arte occidental) teñido, sazonado de Oriente: Como el Medoro del poema. (pp.34–5)

> Even now, if I have to represent the finest image of the boy, in his fullness, I painstakingly reconstruct those days. [...] Sometimes I think that what bound me to Sixto then – what made me so hot for him even, since that is the word for it – was that he was an archetype. That he represented in so lively and exact a manner some very ancient, glorious archetype of beauty. The symmetry, the proportion (the straightness of the nose, the curve of the eyes, his substance, the tactile lips); but added to this perfect canon – like a scarce grain of pepper, a spice which if it distorted the pure flavour really it enriched it, making it more delectable – the dark tone of his skin, the thick black eyelashes, the Moorish air, which to the mere treatise-writer of Doric Greece might not be of value, but which would most certainly be so to the sophists of Syria invoked by the poet Cavafy. You will say that what I'm telling you about has not got very much to do with literature. And if what I've described to you is an absolutely *physical* passion – the fact

that scarcely did I see him than I got an erection – why not also then tell you about this other aspect, which is just as real, and which for me existed and had the weight and substance of some atavistic force? Sixto was the Greek canon of beauty (which the best part of Western Art has ever since pursued) touched and seasoned with the Orient: like Medoro in the poem.

All these different lines of connection both poeticise and eroticise Sixto, and Arturo's narration here finds amid the excess a certain control in the art-historical precision; a control which is curiously empowered by the presence not only of Sixto's body but the recognition of Arturo's blunt physical response to him. Art and lust perform a baroque arabesque and conjure up angels. So when, working on a comparison of Ariosto's and Góngora's poem, Arturo sees Sixto in the lovely moor Medoro he sees an association with the Medoro 'whom Ariosto describes as an "angel of the celestial choirs"' (pp.40–1). In one incident during a ten-day period when they attempt to live together (Carmen has moved out), as Sixto comes back naked from the shower it is 'the sudden visit of an angel which filled me with desire, happiness and disquiet' (p.43); at twenty Sixto evokes (but does not retain) the image of his earlier self, 'a being made of the strange substance of the angels' (p.65). Yet the angelic theme is led back again to the dominion of sex more plainly: having introduced Sixto to Lucía, his next lover, Arturo feels that 'I should have told her, I wanted to, that he had before been even more attractive, that I had experienced genuine shocks of excitement, erections, on seeing him, that he was like certain angelic, but sensual, figures in Italian painting' (p.71).

Although Arturo is not allowed to not know it, the transgressive proximity of art appreciation and an erection, of brute excitement and refined detachment, make Sixto an angel who belongs unequivocally in gay culture: pure sex and pure art, a person and not a person, lust and spirit all at once, the guardian angel of a dissenting point of view. Villena, in a now familiar strategy, is making the angelic the point of intersection of the idealising and the sexualising counter-currents. A transgression which can be seen at work in both the prose and the poetry and which lovingly entwines the cultural and the counter-cultural, the unexpected and the conventional.

The poem 'Acerca de los ángeles en la poesía' ('On Angels in Poetry') in *Death Alone* (*Poesía*, p.325) makes the traditional poetic and Neoplatonic connotations of the word 'angel' lie with the more everyday gay sense of it and reactivates the unresolved movement around and between the two interconnecting zones of the bodily and the imaginary. In this single much-coded word the base and the exalted are confused and inverted:

Al decir *ángel* hacemos una súplica,
pedimos más realidad, y simulando un truco metafísico,
postulamos la plenitud del cuerpo,
la quemazón sanguínea. (No se oculta impureza.)
Hay cuerpos que se compran – pero, claro, amigo –
y hay sordidez y barro, palabras afiladas,
y deslices de sombra . . . (He tocado ceniza.)
Pero también hay cuerpos que se brindan
– y que incluyen el alma en el conjunto –
y asimismo hay sordidez ahí,
con mañanas muy ácidas, y súbitos desencantos
que desmoronan todo
[...]
Al decir *ángel* no se es generoso
ni retórico a secas,
se entiende, solo, que el mundo es imperfecto
pero que hay rastros, señales, rostros
de otra realidad que el saturnal invoca.
Al decir *ángel* se pide muerte, proclamando vida.

When we say *angel* it is in supplication, / we seek yet more reality, and in simulation of some trick of metaphysics, / we postulate the fullness of the body, / the heat in the blood. (Impurity's no secret.) / There are bodies one can buy – but of course, my dear friend! – / and there is squalor, brutish clay, sharp-edged words, / and shadowy slidings away... (I have myself touched ashes.) / But there are bodies which are freely offered too / – and which include the soul into the bargain – and even so there is squalor there, / mornings with a very bitter taste and sudden disappointments / which bring it all tumbling down / [...] / In saying *angel* one is not just being generous / or rhetorical, no more / but simply understanding that the world's imperfect / but there are traces, signs, and countenances / of another world which saturnalia invokes. / In saying *angel* one asks for death while proclaiming life.

The sequence 'traces, signs, and countenances' is significant in the way it links the quest and the encounter, spiritual aspiration and sensory contact. Transcendence comes through the *fiesta* of the senses, and contact with the angels means something emphatically other than dying to the things of this world in a traditional way.

Imperfection is something to be embraced, as a sign of its complement and opposite but also as its palpable self; and, as in 'A Contra-dance', it can eroticise the other reality, charming the metaphysical back down to intersect with sex and be reinscribed in living counter-cultures.

As Prieto (in *Mundo angélico)* and Sahuquillo (in *Cultura homosexual)* show, Spanish angels have frequently allowed transgressive rewritings and conceptual cross-dressings.[2] Sahuquillo reviews the many transgressive signifying practices in which the image of the angel (or, metonymically, just wings) is deployed by writers in the Spanish homosexual tradition (pp.336–46). He emphasises androgyny, the fall of the angel as the coming of spirit into flesh, the association of heaven (via the sky-god Uranus) with Uranianism, angelic purity with homoerotic desire for the naked body, with rebellion against the laws of God and – in Cernuda especially – rebellion against society (*Cultura homosexual*, pp.241–73). In one direction, in Juan Gil-Albert's *Los arcángeles (The Archangels*, published in 1981, but written in 1966) it is a short step from angels to the Ganymede story and High Culture; in another, in Cernuda's poetry, a boy's shoulder-blades can signify wings and sex can become heavenly, but only in a deconstruction of the high cultural and metaphysical connotations of the angelic (pp.341–2). As both Sahuquillo and Villena are (not surprisingly) quick to notice, Cernuda's poem 'Los marineros son las alas del amor' ('Sailors Are The Wings of Love') in *Los placeres prohibidos (Forbidden Pleasures*, 1931) makes the link, in Villena's words, between 'sailors (Beauty), the sea, and love' and 'desire, love and body'.[3] A whole dynamic of disobedience and a widespread counter-cultural network of rebellion against prohibition is activated in an angelic discourse which serves to anchor straight idealisations firmly to the ground of sexuality.

2. The whole transcultural strategy is supported by the felicitous pun available in Spanish on the word 'pluma', 'feather' and, equally luckily, 'quill' and thus 'pen': to have a lot of *pluma* is to be obviously gay or camp; 'gente de pluma' may signify 'writers' and/or camp gay men. Feathers, consequently, are much highlighted in Prieto's drawings in *Mundo angélico*.

3. Villena, 'Introducción', to Luis Cernuda, *Las nubes. Desolación de la Quimera*, ed. Villena, Madrid, 1984, pp.11–57: pp.19–20. See also the visual links in Prieto, *Mundo angélico*, between the sections 'Arcángeles' ('Archangels') pp.41–64 and 'Marineros' ('Sailors') pp.97–124. The line from Cernuda is, inevitably, cited early on (p.99) in this latter section which also includes an extract from an unattributed biography by Juan Ramírez de Lucas describing Prieto wandering around in Italy dressed as a sailor (pp.102–5).

Love's Mystifications

Arturo's placing of the otherwise very ordinary if handsome Sixto in such a discourse of art and angels pulls both of them towards a much more unambiguously gay-oriented arena than the curious and self-deluding utopian sexual space Arturo intends to construct. Having been out of the story for two years, on the coast and the islands of the Mediterranean and in the company of rich older men, Sixto returns one day to have the angelic in him once again firmly linked to the Italianate. One evening Sixto and Arturo meet, and after they have talked a while Sixto leaves. Arturo looks back on the episode and muses:

> Al cerrar la puerta, de repente, pensé en Miguel Angel. Y acudí a sus sonetos, y a reproducciones de sus esculturas y dibujos, y sentí no saber dibujar ni escribir para hablar de ese muchacho que acababa de irse. ¿Febo di Poggio, Tommaso Cavalieri? ¿Era mi historia parecida a alguna de esas, o acaso un poco mezcla de ambas? Hubiera querido poder esbozar su *Victoria* y poner el rostro de Sixto en el muchacho escorzado, y mi cara en la del viejo que, abajo, se doblega. *(Amor Pasión,* pp.59–60)

> Shutting the door behind him, suddenly I thought of Michelangelo. And I got out his sonnets and reproductions of his sculptures and drawings, and I was sorry not to be able to write or to draw so that I could to speak of the boy who had just left. Febo di Poggio? Tommaso Cavalieri? Was my story like these? Or something of a mixture of the two perhaps? I should have liked to sketch his 'Victory' and put Sixto's face to the foreshortened figure of the boy and my own to the old man doubled up beneath.

As we are reminded in *I, Michelangelo Buonarroti*, Febo di Poggio represents a rough, carnal beauty (like the Sixto of the beaches and beds) and Tommaso de Cavalieri the ideal love. In the words of the fictionalised Michelangelo, Febo 'was the adventure of a summer's day,' his body that of 'a young animal, inviting as it entrapped you' *(Buonarroti,* p.157). Cavalieri, whom Villena sees not as the chaste, Platonic friend of conventional bio-criticism (p.159) but the truly ideal lover whose body is clearly sexually enjoyed but (again in words of the fictionalised Michelangelo) is 'the gilded perfection of flesh, its fire, which anticipates paradise,' a body 'in which God had allowed beauty to be reflected' (p.158). In both these forms Arturo finds nostalgia not only for youth but for perfection and wholeness too (like Michelangelo: *Buonarotti*, pp.149–58). Sixto seen from such an angle is eclipsed, scarcely seen at all. Nevertheless, Arturo's avid gaze (watched carefully by César, the recipient of the letter of confession) both fixes Sixto in a position of disenfranchisement and frees him to fly – angelically – off into wonderful and diverse cultural arenas. Although these are initially coded by Arturo and his learning, and although Sixto is framed in this sense, the image of Sixto also shifts into positions out of the control of the Arturo who does not want to recognise his true sexual positionality: Arturo falls into the intellectual lover's trap of allowing sex once culturalised and impassioned to be reconstructed as 'love'.

As the reading César sees, his friend – whose heterosexual life has mirrored his own – moves from having sex, through the 'dark area' of same-sex attraction, to falling in love and this radical shift of subject position is marked, in the third chapter of the story, by Sixto's image seen in photographs (for a second time), in a mirror, and in a last frenzy of cultural framings set – tellingly – in the bedroom and bathroom of the now dead Diego Bassani, epitome of the old-style cultured homosexual.

The transformational sequence begins, three pages on from the passage on Michelangelo, with a party in November 1975 given by Jesús, Bassani's widowed lover, for a double celebration of his own birthday and the death of Franco (*Amor pasión*, pp.64–5). The political change, in a gesture as typical of Villena's dissidence as it is of Arturo's blind infatuation, is quite emptied of meaning by the presence of the newly empowered Sixto. Some photographs taken the morning after the party, while recalling the previous set of Sixto as good-time beach-boy at Benidorm, reverse the image and prompt Arturo to see him now not as a modern pagan sex symbol but 'a being made of the strange substance of the angels' (p.65). Although Sixto has been put out of mind and out of the story for two years which have seen Arturo and Lucía become emotionally and sexually bonded, Arturo again slides into the 'dark area' first acknowledged in the telling of the episode at the café terrace with Bassani. On the strength of their night spent together, and spurred on by the photographs, Arturo agrees to Sixto's request that he take him to a black-tie gala night at a fashionable discothèque.

> Y recordé de súbito, que tiempo antes, me había apetecido vestir bien a Sixto y llevarlo a cenar a buenos restaurantes, como si fuésemos dos

camaradas en no sé qué heterodoxa novela de alta sociedad . . .
Quedamos al día siguiente y acudimos a comprarle un *smoking* [...] Y
a la noche suguiente fui [...] a recogerle [...] me abrió la puerta
sonriendo. Con el pelo negro hacia atrás, reciente mojado, y el *smoking*
negro con las solapas de raso, y los zapatos de charol lucientes, Sixto
se me presentaba en una imagen inusual de galán romántico. (pp.65–
6)

And I remembered suddenly that, before, I had always liked to dress
Sixto up and take him out to dine in good restaurants, as if we were
two companions in some unorthodox high-society novel . . . We
arranged to meet the following day and went off to buy him a dinner-
jacket [...] The next night I went to pick him up [...] he opened the door
to me with a smile. With his black hair slicked back and still wet, and
in his dinner-jacket with satin lapels and shining patent leather shoes,
he presented an unusual image of a dashing romantic hero.

'Unusual', of course, only for the purposes of Arturo's narration,
since the figure in the doorway here stands dead-centre of our
expectations of Arturo's strategies. It fits snugly into a rich if clichéd
context of images of screen stars from Errol Flynn to Antonio
Banderas, as well as fitting the literary backdrop of Scott Fitzgerald
and *The Great Gatsby*, set up in the course of the description of the
night out (p.66).

In the middle of the glamourous gala night – during which the
whole framing process is made more obvious by the presence of
Luis Antonio de Villena himself seen across the dance-floor (p.67)[4]
– Sixto and Arturo bump into one another in the cloakroom and
for fun Sixto asks Arturo to paint a moustache on his face with some
eye-liner:

y simulando estudiar el modo de trazar las líneas, le acaricié un
instante, y le besé después, y él corrspondió en los labios. Fue un
instante – estábamos solos – [...] pero guardo con mucha intensidad
aquella imagen. De *smoking* los dos, esbeltos en el negro, besándonos
frente al espejo del tocador, todo iluminado de focos como un diminuto
escenario. ¿No era una secuencia cinematográfica? Una heterodoxa
escena en una hermosa película *retro* . . . (p.67)

and pretending to work out how to trace the lines, I caressed his face
for a moment, then kissed him, and he kissed me back, on the lips. It
was a moment, no more – we happened to be alone there – [...] but I

4. Villena is clearly identifiable, but only named at the very end of the novella:
p.104.

remember the scene with great intensity. The two of us in dinner-jackets, slim in black, kissing in front of the mirror, all lit by spotlights around it like a miniature stage. Was this not like a sequence from a film? Some off-beat scene out of a beautiful retro-style movie.

This moment of togetherness – both touching and absurd – is pivotal. It acknowledges with disarming self-consciousness Arturo's power over the representations of desire and of Sixto but it is the point, the dark area, at which Arturo begins to be drawn through the reflections of the glass and text to find that the scene of their 'Pygmalionesque' relationship (p.69) has been inverted. It is this mirrored scene and its consequence that compels the reconstruction of identity which is Arturo's decision to write his long letter to César and, along a tortuous route, to come out as gay.

Shortly after this many-framed scene, when the two meet for sex again, Arturo discovers that Sixto has urethritis and this – with touching perversity – is crucial to the development of what is going to be love:

> me sentí súbitamente inundado de una especie de ternura. Pero era una dulzura que no expulsaba al deseo. Y no sé por qué le abracé ruda y suavemente a un tiempo. Y le besé después, fuerte, porque sentí la imperiosa necesidad de que notase mi cariño, el brazo del compañero de placer, el tigre que cuida al tigre, el calor de dos desnudeces entre el boscaje, cuando uno está herido . . . Y poco a poco le fui desabrochando los pantalones. Pero también, y quizá más hondo, sentía una infinita ternura porque parecía comprobar que la perfección, la belleza, es asimismo vulnerable, y sobre el animalillo hermoso y joven podía crecer el verdín y la tizne . . . (pp.73–4)

> I felt suddenly overwhelmed by a kind of tenderness. But this sweet, soft feeling did not exclude desire. And I don't know why but I hugged him, roughly and gently both at once. And afterwards I kissed him, hard, because I urgently wanted him to see my affection, feel about him the arm of a companion in pleasure, a tiger caring for another tiger, the heat of two naked bodies in the undergrowth, when one is wounded . . . And bit by bit I undid his trousers. But I also felt, deeper down maybe, an infinite tenderness because it seemed to be suddenly revealed to me that perfection, beauty, is vulnerable even so, and that verdigris and grime might grow on this young and lovely creature . . .

This scene is an only half-acknowledged sentimental crisis-point for Arturo and the text reveals the strain with the cultural displacements of the image of Sixto coming in even swifter succession than in the gala-night scenes. The image of wounded tiger-cub companion dissolves into the suggestion 'Why don't you take a bath? Go on, you can be the young Roman patrician, and I'll be the slave at the baths . . .' (p.74). After the bath Arturo turns carer, putting aside sexual desire: 'I held back. I now think I don't know why, but I held back' (p.75). The scene is allowed a Romantic operatic pathos as he even toys with the thought 'Who knows to what degree of passion or intimacy of feeling we might have been led had we shared [...] the infection?' (p.75). There is a double-edged intimacy in the presentation of Sixto's symptoms: 'from the end of his glans there emerged, yellowish and acid, a rare gum, a bad pearl' (p.74); it points both to the plain sore facts and to a decadent aestheticism which in its customary way moves simultaneously away from and disturbingly close to direct engagement with the object of desire in the use of the morbid close-up to create a thrill of alienation.

This whole episode is straightforwardly emotive, and even the traces of defensive homophobic vacillation in Arturo add pathos: he feels tenderness, but of course lust too, like a Real Man, but he has also let us see this weakness. Leaving Sixto tucked up in bed Arturo leaves money (for antibiotics, but tacitly too as if to pay for the scene) on the bedside table just as a mother or a fond brother might leave a glass of water: again he is both justifying the behaviour to himself (real men sleep with prostitutes) and displaying an emotional involvement. Similarly destabilising are the now only thinly self-deceiving disavowals which punctuate the narrative here: Arturo says twice 'I don't know why but [...]', refers to 'a kind of tenderness' and notes how the vulnerability of Sixto's beauty 'seemed to be revealed'. The fact is, as anyone but Arturo can see, that he has fallen in love.

As the story goes on and Sixto grows older and less perfect, compassion reconstructs all the desire, fondness, camaraderie and evasions finally as true love. This much is revealed after a reading-time of only half an hour but two years in story-time, with Sixto nearly twenty-four and about to finish his military service. Arturo sees how he has filled out, and is looking 'somewhat unkempt' (p.86): 'I noticed some little folds his skin made on his neck, under the ears, and which were not really all that obvious but I saw and felt them to be like the swansong of youth, like the dying of a handsome hero of ancient times' (p.86). This decline is linked, in the very ordinary context of a gay bar on a weekday night and talk of escapades at the barracks, to further renaissance and baroque literary treatments of the theme of the fading rose. The linkage is both an evasion of Arturo's true feelings and a confirmation, and once more the framing of desire has a way of generating the very reactions it had sought to control. As emotion ousts mere reference the figure of Sixto refuses to be distanced and exalted to symbolic status:

> Sixto no era el de antes [...] Era un ser menos brillante. Ahora en ese momento, ya era mortal. *Marchite ¡oh! nunca frío y cano hielo / de tus labios la dulce y blanda rosa.* Y empecé a sentir una especie de compasión hacia él [...] era un sentimiento ciertamente distinto. No me excitaba ni me sentía dentro del haz de luz de lo maravilloso. Simplemente me turbaba y me daba pena. Pero era una pena *atractiva*, si puedo decirlo, algo que me hacía, metafóricamente, tender los brazos hacia él, querer protegerlo, intentar cuidarlo. (p.86)[5]

> Sixto was not the same as before [...] He was a less radiant being. At this moment he was, now, mortal. *'Let not, oh never, hoary-headed cold make fade / the sweet soft rose, your lips.'* And I began to feel a kind of compassion for him [...] a quite different feeling. I was not excited, nor did I feel myself to be moving now within the circle of miraculous light. It was just that he perturbed me, and I felt pity for him. But it was a pity that had *attractions*, if I can put it that way, something which made me, metaphorically, reach out my arms towards him, protect him, try to look after him.

The body – emotion – establishes its own theatre of metaphorical action but with the strong memory in the text here of that previous scene of the wounded Sixto where the physical was so insistent. The evasive use of the qualifying 'a kind of . . .' (employed too in the previous scene) fails to prevent the slippage from framing to involvement. The metaphorical urge to protect is retrospectively made real by the memory of the physical embrace and the *'attractions'* of pity are informed by the physical excitements of the lovemaking of the preceding pages. In one direction there is this pulling away from the figurative and the exalted, in another a resistance in the text to losing the metaphysical in Sixto, and it is this dynamic of vacillation which constructs love. Despite the banality of the scenes which are unfolding, the special and idealising status of the relationship comes back insistently:

---

5. The quotation is the opening line of Franciso de Rioja (1583?–1659), 'Soneto V'.

yo había prestado solo un mecánico y aparente interés a la trivial conversación, cuando Sixto nos dijo que si le invitábamos a comer algo, pues estaba sin cenar, y tenía hambre. Y como a esas horas sólo se podía comer en un *Drugstore*, hacia allá salimos [...] Nos sentamos, Sixto pidió un *plato combinado*, y Jesús y yo, un par de ginebras nuevamente. Y allí, mientras la charla seguía – bastante intranscendente – la compasión que el muchacho me produjo se fue incrementando. Hubiera querido – pero no lo hice – tomar su mano y acariciarla, y decirle que era hermoso (y ciertamente lo era) aunque yo supiera que había cambiado, que le faltaba carisma, y que todo se iría – yo lo notaba – irremediablemente cuesta abajo . . . Me hubiera gustado detener el tiempo para él. (pp.86–7)

I had been paying only apparent and mechanical attention to the trivial conversation when Sixto suggested we invite him to have something to eat, since he hadn't had supper yet and was hungry. And since at that time of night the only place to eat was in a *Drugstore*, that's where we went [...] We sat down and Sixto ordered a chef's platter, and Jesús and I two more gins. And there, as the talk – somewhat insignificant as it was – went on, the pity this boy inspired in me grew stronger and stronger. I should have liked to – but did not – take his hand and caress it and tell him he was handsome (which indeed he was) although I knew he had changed, that he lacked charisma now, and that everything – I realized – was irredeemably set on a downward path . . . I should have liked to make time stop for him.

Sixto does not stay with them that night, but rather desperately goes off in search for a blond and very beautiful sixteen-year old for whom he has fallen: 'He was bringing his story full circle (and perhaps we all end up doing the same)' (p.88). This, and the change in Sixto, closes the sentimental circle too, with a recapitulation and final development of the trajectories and terminologies of the affair, and of all affairs. Arturo obsessively reworks his theme, resurrecting aspects of his feelings towards Sixto through denials of them, weaving from one position to another, in and out of simplicity, in and out of intricate idealisations:

días más tarde, o esa noche misma, pensaba: Quisiera detener el tiempo para él, quisiera eternizarlo, quisiera vivir con él eternamente, para siempre, siempre, si él fuera siempre tal y como yo le había conocido . . . Porque el sentimiento que ahora me inspiraba aquel Sixto (y que de alguna manera resumía o refundía todos los anteriores) no era, obviamente, aquel deslumbramiento, aquel fogonazo ante el esplendor, ante el enjoyado abismo de la Belleza; ni era tampoco la ternura confraternal y guerrera del compañerismo, ni el afecto corporal y pasional que brota de la *virtus* de los camaradas. Era un sentimiento amalgamado de frustración, de cariño, de ternura, de paz, de compasión, de deseo físico, de perduración más allá de las contingencias . . . ¿Cómo llamarlo? No lo supe en ese momento [...] Y poco a poco, en los días que siguieron a aquel fugaz encuentro – días por lo demás normales, en que acudí a la Facultad, y salí una noche con Lucía mientras una chica se quedaba con el niño – acerté con el nombre. Mi sentimiento (¡qué extraño darme cuenta entonces!) tenía un nombre, un nombre común, manido, tópico, sobre el que se habían vertido – y se vertirían – ríos, cántaros de tinta, pero que cada cual descubre como fenómeno único e irrepetible, personalísimo. *Amor* era ese nombre. De repente al verle distinto, yo me había dado cuenta que amaba a Sixto, que lo quería y que le había querido desde la primera y lejana vez – más de ocho años – en que le viera en un paseo, al final del verano, buscando, como un hermoso animal salvaje, el dinero para seguir viviendo, y a ser posible, seguir gozando . . . Yo le había amado siempre, pero sólo ahora, entonces, cuando era ya todo imposible, cuando yo lo sentía ya como imposible, me daba cuenta. (pp.88–9)

days later, or that same night, I thought: I wish I could stop time for him, make him eternal, live with him eternally, for ever and always, if he could always be just how I had known him . . . Because the feeling inspired in me by this new Sixto (who in some way resumed and revised all the previous Sixtos) was not, obviously, the blaze of light, that starburst in the presence of splendour, before the jewelled abyss of Beauty, nor was it the tenderness of warriors and brothers which comes of companionship, nor the passionate and physical attachment which comes of the *virtus* of comrades. It was a feeling made up of frustration, affection, tenderness, peace, compassion, physical desire, of living on beyond the accidents of the present . . . What to call it? Just at that moment I didn't know [...] And little by little in the days following that brief encounter – days which were otherwise quite normal, when I went into the department, and one night went out with Lucía and left the child with a babysitter – I hit upon the name for it. This feeling of mine had a name, a common, well-worn, ordinary name over which pitchers, rivers of ink had been and would yet be spilled but which each discovers as a unique and unrepeatable, highly personal phenomenon. *Love* was its name. Suddenly I had realised, seeing him look so different, that I loved Sixto; that I had loved him from that first and distant time when eight years back I had seen him on a boulevard at the end of summer, hunting, like a wild and lovely animal, for the money to go on with life and, if possible, to go on relishing it . . . I had loved him always, but only now – or then – when it was all impossible, and when I felt it indeed to be so, did I come to realise this.

That uncertain shift from 'now' to 'then' shows that there are two belated realisations: one that this was love, and the other that it must be given recognition and articulation through the writing of the letter to César. The gap between the two positions, occupied by those 'normal' days of work and family life, is the fissure made by the instabilities of his sexuality and his failure to take up a truly dissident position by surrendering to what is not just a gay love but *amour passion*, an extra-social, anti-conventional, counter-cultural engagement of the self.

Between the narration of the wounded Sixto scene and that of the *Drugstore* scene, between the infusion of pity and tenderness and their late recasting as love, Arturo turns in a measured way to a conventional heterosexual sex-life and to domestic love. During the two-year gap he resists the charms of an elegant Italian boy while away at a conference in Rome, has 'a little adventure' with a woman research student from Barcelona, and becomes oppressed by middle-class guilt and anxiety about having children, the difficulty of finding a home help and child care, and 'other little problems' (pp.79–82). He rediscovers a kind of love for Lucía.

> estaba muy bien con ella. Me apetecía ese cuerpo, que lentamente volvió a su estado normal, y que yo conocía hasta en sus menores detalles. Sus pliegues y sus fosas. Pero me apetecía, y mucho. Suponía, supongo, que eso es el amor. Lo que la inmensa mayoría de la gente denomina amor. Una profunda unión interna, íntima, casi incontable, basada, desde luego, en la búsqueda de compañía, de calor, en la huída de la soledad, y naturalmente en miles de necesidades cotidianas, y junto a ese bienestar, junto a ese estar a gusto, una cierta atracción sexual ocasional, gozosa, sin tabúes, y sin sorpresas, en cuerpos que se compenetran bien, y que llegan a ser un poco como llave y cerradura – y no importa quién sea quién – siempre en la misma puerta. Algo, en suma, enormemente difícil y profundo, pero también ¿a qué no añadirlo?, enormemente trivial, fácil, cotidiano, inmenso bloque de mármol sin brillo. Eso era y es (con sus alzas y bajas) el amor que tenemos. El *amor perfecto*, estarán dispuestos a sancionar muchos, porque además la unión era libre y nadie legalmente nos ataba. (pp.82–3)

It was really good with her. I was attracted to that body as it slowly returned to its usual state and which I knew in the smallest details. Its folds and hollows. But it attracted me, and greatly. I supposed, and suppose now, that this was love. What the vast majority call love. A deep, inner union, an intimacy which is almost impossible to describe, based, of course, on the need for company, warmth, the flight from solitude, and, naturally, on a thousand and one little daily needs; and along with this sense of well-being, a certain casual, joyful, taboo-free sexual attraction, with no surprises and between two bodies which are well-matched to each other and end by being rather like a lock and key – it doesn't matter who is which – always in the same familiar door. Something, then, hugely difficult and profound, but also – and why not say this too? – hugely trivial, easy, routine, a vast block of unpolished marble. This – with its ups and downs – is the love that we had and have. *Perfect love*, as many would be glad to agree, since our union was moreover a free one and there was nobody to tie us down legally.

However, in the text there is the inevitable deconstruction of the comfortable forms of love. The image of the raw block of marble shouts out the lack of the chiselling of idealism, perfection, sculpted beauty. Its frigidity, however, also challenges the cosiness of the familiar with the bluntness of harsh truth. Despite the confident little image of the key and the door deployed by Arturo, opening the 'same familiar door' is going to show that the intended contrast of *agape* against *eros* will not serve as a tidy dualistic aid to definition and decision. Sensing the difficulties of such a collapse into one another of his terms he takes refuge in narration: 'But I don't want to reflect so much on all this, rather to tell you the story' (p.83). However, the tale of a whole year, the first year of the baby's life, lasts scarcely half a page and has only one marked event in it – a talk with Lucía about the Sixto affair. A talk which leads at once back into reflection:

> esta breve conversación la tuvimos en la cama bisbiseando para no despertar al niño [...] Lucía me acarició, yo la acaricié después, despacio, notando un grato calor en aquel tacto tan mío, tan *familiar*, y entendí esa palabra de repente. ¿Era eso el amor? ¿El amor es tu vida con Marie, y la mía con Lucía? No voy a hacer distingos, ni sutiles matices. El amor es *eso*, exactamente. El ágape matrimonial (se esté o no casado) la búsqueda profunda de dos seres, su íntima resistencia a la agresión de la vida . . . (pp.83–4)

> we had this short conversation in bed, whispering so as not to wake the child [...] Lucía caressed me and afterwards I caressed her, slowly, finding a pleasant warmth in a contact which was so much my own, so *familiar*; and I suddenly understood the word. Was this perhaps then love? Is love your life with Marie, and mine with Lucía? I'm not going to enter into subtle distinctions here. Love is just that, no more no less.

The *agape* of marriage (whether one is married or not), two beings searching each other out profoundly, their intimate resistance to life's many aggressions.

On the one hand there is this resistance to subtle distinctions; on the other in this whole development of Arturo's sense of love there is the now accustomed ebb and flow of shifts and substitutions within the terms, of parenthetical precisions and asides which is his (and Villena's) style.

By reading and by brooding Arturo has framed his feelings impossibly and been framed by his text, made to romanticise, to fail to communicate with Sixto, to mystify himself and misplace the true intensity of life. This, in part, is César's reading. Sixto, like Arturo, ends up in a relationship with a woman and with a son, desirous of stability, 'order and peace and quiet' (p.102). Arturo's part of the story ends with an evasive return to the securities of the everyday – 'I am happy, moderately happy, with my son, with Lucía, my books and friends, conventionally happy too, why not say it?' (p.94). A long essay, in the last chapter of his 'letter', on the incompatibility of *eros* with human relationships also seals his story (pp.91–4). So too does a petty and bourgeois worry about the young not giving a thought to tomorrow which prefaces his final meditations:

No quiero parecer un moralista adusto y sentencioso [...] Quisiera en todo caso que estas palabras [...] hagan patente que la gran felicidad [...] la inmensa felicidad no existe. O existe, sí, como desgarrón repentino, como hermoso tirón que ciega, como flecha que entra por los ojos [...] una herida, una turbación que uno teme y desea al mismo tiempo. Que ojalá vuelva, y que no vuelva nunca. No sé. Nadie sabe. Y quizá sea mejor no pensar en ello. (p.94)

I do not wish to appear a severe, pedantic moralist [...] I want these words to [...] make it plain that great happiness [...] immense joy does not exist. Or does, as a sudden wrenching, lovely, force which draws you and blinds like an arrow entering the eye [...] a wound and a disruption which one both desires and fears. If only it would come once more, or if only never come. I do not know. Nobody knows. And perhaps it is best not to dwell on it.

So the uncertainty of identification which has energised his whole story still persists; is he or is he not an outsider? His lyricism – the language which makes love – moves us because it is such a transparently belying counterpoint to his express intent and to his decision. Although the option for 'moderate', 'conventional' happiness is allowed convincing development and is crystalised in the name of *agape*, the fire and the intensity of the language of *eros* and the whole dynamic of Arturo's story casts the focus elsewhere. What is meant to be a warning (or is it?) turns out to be a seduction as we remember the bitter-sweet intensities of the story. The reading César, for his part, is led into wistful meditations which also place special value on what is lost:

> todo daba la razón a Arturo. Sixto sin saberlo, renegaba de la pasión, del *eros*, porque sólo un héroe (como el Tristán wagneriano) puede admitir y querer ser destruido. Y todos – por diversas sendas – terminábamos cobijándonos en el próximo (en nuestra mujer, en los amigos) como una forma agradable de supervivencia. Todos parecíamos saber que el horizonte es falso, es decir, que el *otro lado* exige nuestra claudicación y nuestra desaparición absoluta. Noté que Arturo (tras narrarme lo dicho) estaba triste, vagamente melancólico. Y a mí me fue contagiando la melancolía. Quizá porque vi – como la literatura avisa – qué distinto era todo de cuanto se había leído. Que la pasión es siempre romántica y caediza, y que por un Lord Byron hay novecientos noventa y nueve Tennyson. Esto es, frente a un héroe *perdedor*, una comitiva de *instalados*. Y todos – hasta Sixto que aún no lo era – me parecían ya *instalados*: empezando por mí mismo. (p.102)

Arturo was absolutely right. Without knowing it, Sixto turned his back on passion, the passion of *eros*, because only a hero (like the Wagnerian Tristan) can allow himself and want himself to be destroyed. And we all, along our different paths, end up taking shelter in what is close to home (in our wife, in our friends) as a cosy form of survival. We all seemed to realise that the horizon is false, that is to say that to be on the *other side* requires an abandonment of ourselves, our absolute annihilation. I noticed that Arturo, when he had told me all this, was sad and vaguely melancholy. And the melancholy affected me as well. Perhaps because I saw – as literature tells us – how different it all was to what one had read. Saw that passion is always romantic and unsteady. That for every Lord Byron there are nine hundred and ninety-nine Lord Tennysons. That is, set against each heroic *loser*, a retinue of the socially *well-placed*. And everyone – even Sixto, who as yet was not so – seemed to me to be well-placed and settled: starting with myself.

Nevertheless, despite the comfort sought by Arturo in his sexual-political evasions and narratorial vacillations, and in a cunningly paradoxical way actually because of his literary mystifications, he is not entirely the disaffected and compromising ex-dissenter César represents in him. Part of his problem of sentimental identification is not induced by literature at all but by conventions of heterosexual and bourgeois society, for he has made the error of the false and separating distinction between a familiar, warm love which must dwell in the realm of domestic, loving intimacy and the blazing fire of passionate love which must reside absolutely elsewhere:

> yo no sabía entonces si fuera de eso y de la concreta pasión física por un cuerpo – perecedera – había algo más. Yo no lo sabía. Porque tampoco mi relación con Sixto la sacaba del terreno de la excepción, de lo ocasional, de lo insólito, y ahí, obviamente, me equivocaba. Una equivocación múltiple, uno de cuyos más erróneos brazos era no unir la palabra *amor* con la voz *insólito*, o con la más benévola de *ocasional*. (p.84)

> I did not know then whether beyond all this and the concrete physical – and fleeting – passion for a body there was anything more. I simply did not know. Because I never took my relationship with Sixto beyond the realms of the exceptional, the temporary, the extraordinary; and there, obviously, lay my mistake. A multiple error, one of whose erroneous branches was the failure to link the word *love* with the word *extraordinary*, or even with the more benign word *occasional*.

Literature and sentimental idealisation offer a way of reconciling the forms of love for Arturo but they also undermine the passionate, the dissident element which in Villena's terms is necessary for love's passionate fulfilment. Arturo's is a counter-cultural lesson which he thoroughly fails to learn and which only the real outsiders, we readers, see in its true frame, the dissident cultural frame Villena is constructing in his writing but which eludes both his narrators. Arturo betrays the quality of difference in his feelings by inscribing Sixto excessively into his world of high culture and middle-class, straight concerns; César betrays Arturo by failing to rescue from the letter its potential radical content, rewriting the love story as a rueful recognition of his own lack of courage. Their linked roles in the telling and enacting of this tale and their common capitulation to the demands and discourses of conventional behaviour and expression make it, in part, a story of male bonding. As such it excludes, evades, and fears homosexual love, threatening to write Sixto out of his own story.

5

Bonding and Collusion

Friends: Comrades: Lovers

*I*n *Amour Passion*, as Arturo's story progresses, a curiously ordinary grand narrative develops to ground the extravagant flights of aesthetic coding, emotional exaltation and sexual obfuscation. It is the story of Perfect Friendship. The myth of untrammelled, transparent communication with Another, who is your image, your ideal, your bulwark against loneliness and emptiness, and above all the continuation of and connection to a past you probably never had.

Middle- to highbrow Spanish narrative writing and art cinema of the past quarter century has been obsessed with narrating a way out of present uncertainties, sexual and political, back into an adolescence or a childhood cosily wrapped about in the certainties of family, safe friendships, familiarity and, often, a more or less idyllic provincial existence.[1] Villena turns this nostalgia and the grand friendship narrative through the angles of homoerotic desire to reflect this cultural wishfulness perversely and couples the Spanish obsession with the days of youth with the intertwining cultures and practices of homosociality and homosexual brotherliness.[2] What he is concerned to narrate is the reverse of the

1. The tradition is represented by texts such as Ana María Matute's much reissued *Primera memoria* (1959: translated, as *School of the Sun*, by Elain Kerrigan, New York, 1963), Carmen Martín Gaite's *Retahilas* (*Story-lines*, 1974) and the 1990 winner of the Premio Nadal, Juan José Millás's *La soledad era esto* (*So This Was Solitude*); also Víctor Erice's *El espíritu de la colmena* (*The Spirit of the Beehive*, 1973) and *El Sur* (*The South*, 1983). One notable exception in narrative is Rosa Chacel's *La insolación* (*Sunstroke*, 1963) where adolescence is marked as a site for sexual transgression.

2. The term 'homosocial' is adapted and developed by Eve Sedgwick in *Between Men: English Literature and Homosocial Desire*, New York, 1985: '"Homosocial" is a word occasionally used in history and the social sciences, where it describes the social bonds between persons of the same sex; it is a neologism, obviously formed by analogy with "homosexual" and just as obviously meant to be distinguished from "homosexual". In fact, it is applied to such activities as "male bonding",

cultural norm, an escape from the certainties and securities of life after twenty-one back to a sexually-charged and family-free vitality which, though it often will be sited in the country or at the beach, gets its cultural and erotic charge very much from the metropolitan scene.

When Arturo sees Sixto after a two-year absence another small physical imperfection prompts a flight of nostalgia in him which goes precisely in Villena's subversive direction. He notices that Sixto's teeth, always poor, are becoming more decayed (a theatrically obvious sign of his passage through time towards imperfection) (*Amor Pasión*, p.62). Sixto tells him that a 'friend he had been staying with in Menorca' had promised him some money to pay for dental treatment, but they had split up and the money was never forthcoming:

> Pensé entonces (aunque nada dije) que un día yo debería hacer ese regalo al chico. Y al decirme mentalmente esa frase, se me coló, como por algún extraño entresijo, nuevamente la palabra *amigo*. Ya he dicho que la belleza – una belleza más juvenil – era rotunda, pero yo empezaba a sentirme como un muchacho que ama confraternalmente a otro, que es su amigo [...] Pero me gustaba mucho, eso era cierto. Y además había algo por debajo, algo que trascendía lo físico, que no era amor, y que, a mi juicio, se parecía sobre todo a la amistad. Pero a una amistad – no sabía bien cómo explicarle – a una amistad de muchachos, era como si su presencia me rejueneciese o más exactamente me adolescentizase. Me sentía con él – dije riendo – como un chico que un día de verano se dispone con su amigo (quince años, pantalones cortos, mucho sexo) a saltar a hurtadillas la tapia de un huerto para robar albaricoques o higos y comérselos después, juntos, reidores, revueltos, a la sombra densa de los árboles, junto al río, en el tórrido calor de las primeras horas de la tarde . . . (p.62)

> I thought then (although I said nothing) that one day I ought to give him the money as a gift. And as I thought this, as if through some strange crack, the word *friend* slipped into my thoughts once more. I have already said that at this stage his beauty – his more youthful beauty – was totally involving, but I was beginning to feel like a young

---

which may, in our society, be characterized by intense homophobia, fear and hatred of homosexuality. To draw the "homosocial" back into the orbit of "desire", of the potentially erotic, then, is to hypothesize the potential unbrokenness of a continuum between homosocial and homosexual — a continuum whose visibility, for men, in our society, is radically disrupted.' (*Between Men*, pp.1–2). See also Woods, *Articulate Flesh*, Part I passim, for examples of homoerotic bonding in poetry.

lad who loves another like a brother, another who is his special friend. [...] But I was very attracted to him, it's true. And there was something else, deeper down, something that went beyond the physical, which was not love, and which to my mind seemed above all to be like friendship. But a friendship – I didn't properly know how to explain it to him – a boyhood friendship; it was as if his presence took me back to my early youth or, rather, to my adolescence. With him I felt – I told him, laughing – like a boy on a summer's day who sets out with his friend (fifteen, in shorts, and lots of sex) to climb over the meadow wall to steal apricots and eat them afterwards together, laughing and tussling, in the dense shade of trees by a river in the torrid heat of the early afternoon . . .

As is characteristic of Arturo, and of the classic buddy scenario, this recognition of tenderness has to be half explained away, as a slip of – or actually here 'into' – the mind, as something other than what it is; and the influx of the name *friendship* requires the compensatory strategy of the construction of a scene of innocent naughtiness and horseplay in the (albeit sultry pastoral) outdoors to bounce it back into appropriate shape.[3] As is characteristic of Villena though, the sensuality of the text heads off any buddy-buddy evasiveness. This idyllic scene – how many allegorical paintings might not these two be modelling? – is a richly encoded space invoked in many of his meditations on the kind of eroticised friendship which brushes up against the spiritual but also quickens the pulse of lust. By amalgamating so many of the geographies of sex – utopian spaces onto which, in the name of an ostensibly desired primitive simplicity, relations of submission and domination may be inscribed by the culture of the empowered[4] – Arturo, and, as we shall be seeing shortly, the two narrators of *Beyond the World* set in motion a difficult dynamic whereby male bonding both cancels out and confirms, in pendulum-driven progress, the oppression of the object of desire. As Eve Sedgwick observes, 'in any male-dominated society, there is a special relationship between male (*including* homosexual) desire and the structures for maintaining and transmitting patriarchal power' (*Between Men*, p.25). Probing in order to soften and cross

3. See Woods, *Articulate Flesh*, pp. 71–7, 'Sportsmanship', for examples of sexually encoded horseplay.
4. Teresa de Lauretis, 'The violence of rhetoric: Considerations on representation and gender', in de Lauretis (ed.), *Technologies of Gender*, Bloomington, 1987, pp.43–4 on Lotman.

the gap in the 'radically disrupted continuum [...] between sexual and non-sexual male bonds' (p.23), Villena's narrators can restructure the relationship, exclude the woman (more or less 'violently') and foist a close cousin of patriarchal power on the object of desire, the boy, the innocent, the gazed-at and iconised. They can perpetuate the asymmetry in the relations of power. But they can in the same gesture also elide the differences between the lover and the one loved, making the boys framed by desire into empowered protagonists in various texts: empowered within the narrative itself (they say yes or no and where to go and when), within the body of the text (the language is so much in thrall to them), and empowered by their ability to escape the more ridiculous, self-deluding movements of intellectualised desire. They are inscribed into gay cultures, into sites of decadence, pleasure and excitement but also gain access to the real advantages these bring (sex, adulation, easy living, advancement even). On the other hand, though, they will simultaneously also be the subordinate, as dependent on written tokens in their text-lives as they would be on the absence of violence and the presence of pesetas or affection in street-life.[5]

In the poems on male 'friendship' the ambivalence of these elisions creates a certain moral opacity: it is hard to pin-point the speaker, and the object of desire is rarely articulated in action and if seen, not heard. The added excitement, heightened in the verse, of the text itself becoming the object of desire – a body – further complicates the structures of power relation (as pleasure has a habit of doing). The following extract from the poem 'Sobre el dios de Homero' ('On Homer's God') in *To Flee from Winter* (*Poesía*, pp.258–60) dramatises the seduction by the text of the reader and, by linking the pleasures of the body and of the text, constructs the object of desire as a controlling subject.

> Se puede decir de muchas cosas. Puedes aplicar
> el nombre (y lo aplicas) a menudo. Pero lo que
> la Belleza verdaderamente es lo sabe sólo el corazón
> cuando se arrastra, cuando tiembla ante la forma hermosa,
> y quisiera pararse allí, acampar para siempre
> en ese oasis, olvidar el destino, contemplando, bebiendo,

---

5. Representations of homosexual relationships in Spanish are overwhelmingly power asymmetrical: see Smith, *Laws*, passim; and especially pp.129–62 for readings of older man-younger man dynamics in the cinema of Eloy de la Iglesia.

nutriéndose de esa armonía que hace suspirar al alma.
[...]
                              Contigo
sería la excursión, el fuego, el cántico nocturno,
la mañana del río – tus piernas dejando aromas
de verano – ahí la sinrazón, los dioses, la alegría;
Malasia que aproxima en tu vientre aventuras,
las selvas, los cafés para copiar apuntes, yo
tus mismos ojos, tú el amor, así la amistad,
el deseo ahí, allí la voz fratria, el placer

                                                              (p.259)

It can be said of many things. You can apply / the name (and do) with frequency. But what Beauty / truly is, that only the heart knows / when it drags itself helpless, trembling before the comely form, / and would stop there, pitch camp for ever / in this oasis, forget destiny and contemplate, drink / and feed on this harmony which makes the soul sigh / [...] With you / it would be a blazing fire, excursions, night song, / the river at morning – your thighs leaving traces of the smells / of summer – there would unreason be, and gods, and happiness; / a Malaysia of adventures promised in your stomach's flesh / forests, copying class notes over cups of coffee, I / as your eyes, you as love itself, friendship as this, / and desire there, there the voice of brotherhood and pleasure.

This friendship, based in ordinary school-day things, is conceptually very far-flung, tensed across many discourses. Clean-edged Neoplatonism shares textual space with the almost morbidly erotic: the heart's trembling and the soul's sighing – otherwise clichés of the discourse of spiritualised love – are ridden of their purity by the decadent 'drags itself' and the hedonistic 'drink and feed on' (though in these details we are not far from the perplexing apparently sensual mysticism of passages of St John of the Cross's *Cántico espiritual*, which may be what suggests the phrase 'cántico nocturno', 'night song'). The night spent in the healthy outdoors (perhaps realistically enough) becomes a sexual interlude of considerable poetic and erotic sophistication, the stock image of the 'smells of summer' is reinvigorated by the transgressive context of the post-orgasmic young male body and is spread across the realms of ecstasy, high myth and lived experience in the extraordinary triad 'unreason [...], and gods, and happiness'. The Malaysia of adventures with its forests is an image whose daring is only increased by its rubbing shoulders with the cosiness of late-night homework. Friendship and the unnamed boy (later in the poem straighforwardly a god) are bestowed with codings in abundance, like all those otherwise ordinary relationships with Sixto, or Gonzalo, or Santi. Desire makes poetry and sex exalted equals.

In *As To A Foreign Place* the poem 'Hermosos rostros del pasado' ('Lovely Faces from the Past') (*Lugar extraño*, pp.39–41) remembers and refigures the characters from *Boys* as 'imágenes doradas de la literatura' ('golden images of literature') but also 'lo que mucho más vale: / Imagen de la vida' (p.40: 'what is worth much more: / The image of life'). The poem thus claims for the companionship of youth and for the wildness of fresh desire the capacity to transcend mere memory and, lovely though its images are, to go beyond the literature of conventional nostalgia. In doing so it rewrites two previous gay elegiac poems, Cernuda's grim 'Apologia pro vita sua' in *Como quien espera el alba* (*As One Who Awaits the Dawn*, 1947: Cernuda, *Poesía*, pp.307–11) and Brines's harshly melancholy 'Todos los rostros del pasado' ('All the Faces of the Past') in *Palabras a la oscuridad* (*Words for the Darkness*: Brines, *Poesía*, pp.115–16). Villena's invocation of a brotherhood of friends and lovers leads in a different direction to these (which find resounding emptiness on looking back). At the poem's climax, the reassertion of the body (as sex, as life) leads away from the painful earlier weighing up of pain and joy, goodness and sorrow and away too from the serenity invoked by Brines and longed for by Cernuda. It leads to a very different, very familiar kind of quietness and ecstasy, conjuring up seductively an intense moment of pleasure:

> ese instante pequeño (y moriremos)
> en que un bello cuerpo grita que se ha parado el mundo,
> y que todo – todo absolutamente – vivirá así de quieto,
> como si el orbe fuese solo presente eterno.
>
> (*Lugar extraño*, p.41)

> that tiny instant (and so we shall die) / in which a lovely body cries out that the world has stopped, / and when everything – all, absolutely all – will live on quiet as this, / as if the whole orb were just eternal present.

In *Beyond The World*, in counterpoint to its obsession with decadence and death, the narrative makes extensive use of the body as 'the image of life' in a particular erotic perspective. One of the ill-starred hero Álvaro's experiments with excess is immersion in the cult of the body and gym culture. Typically

Álvaro's experiment is inspired by reading, in this case Montherlant's *Les Olympiques*, read with 'a fervour which – as was customary with him – went beyond just Montherlant alone' (*Fuera del mundo*, p.88). 'As if by magic, he had stopped smoking and taking drugs, but helped by certain books suggested by I don't know who – if by anyone at all – he began to develop what I shall call ideals of a chivalric and heroic Greece' (p.89).

His friend Carlos is, in alternate chapters of the book, a narrator akin to the slightly prudish and distant, jealous narrator of some of the tales in *Boys*: he declines to be drawn into the fantasies. At the gym Álvaro meets Javier (three years his senior at twenty-two), who is a bronzed innocent, neither an intellectual nor a poetic match for Álvaro. The book's other, unnamed narrator (whose point of view and experiences are, again, both close and not close to those of Luis Antonio de Villena) has a lyrical but straightforward explanation for the attraction between the two young men which undercuts Álvaro's own idealisations while in a way still recognisably exalting the muscle cult:

> Pero ¿cómo brota una relación que se apoya en la cultura del cuerpo? Por narcisismo, naturalmente. Las miradas mutuas tienen que lamer los cuerpos con una suavidad que en ningún caso se confunda con lo femenino (dos hombres juntos deben odiar lo femíneo), y de esa lengua cálida hacer surgir fuerza, autocomplacencia. Un refocile en la espuma del grito, del músculo tenso, de las flexiones que aumentan en número, el orgasmo lento del propio placer espejado. (pp.89–90)

> But, how does a relationship based on body culture come about? Through narcissism, naturally. Those mutual gazes must lick over the bodies with a smoothness that on no account should be confused with femininity (two men together are obliged to hate all that is feminine), and from those hot tongue-strokes must come strength, a self-sufficient pleasure. A hot surge of feeling in the spittle-flecked cries of effort, in tensed muscle, press-ups increasing in number, the slow orgasm of self-pleasure mirrored back.

There is an equivocal sexual-political awareness in the wry observation about the special homophobic-homoerotic bind which men together weave about them in homosocial practices and desires. The nouns – despite an adventurously poetical context in both rhythm and adjective – are porn-story commonplaces and as such eroticise the text brutally and make its idealisations less cerebral, much less bookish, than would usually be suggested either by the Spartan-cum-Greco-Roman or the Aesthetic-Excessive discourses which overlay the episode.

Unlike the impositions of coding made by Arturo on Sixto, which at least ostensibly allow the latter to float through a number of different discursive areas (Art, friendship, angelhood, comradeship, love), the construction of the Álvaro-Javier relationship fixes it in closed arenas of association. If they wrestle, it is Roman wrestling (p.92); when they have four-way sex with two women-friends of Javier's they only discuss it gruffly over post-shower whiskies in coarse (and sexist) terms enclosed in the discourse of Real Men (p.96); and, in a passage in free indirect style, Álvaro is seen to emphasise the primitive and uncomplicated in Javier in a way which on any other terms would be a form of superiorist objectification:

> estaba aureolado del saludable encanto de lo primitivo, de lo que se deja ir río abajo, y es feliz. Javi le atrapaba como una onda íntima, y tenía la sensación (cuando luchaban, cuando hacían flexiones y miraban la humedad y la destreza de los músculos) que habían vivido juntos mucho tiempo: piratas peleando en mares ajenos, soldados que lustraban por la noche, al fuego de la amistad, sus corazas. (p.97)

> around him there was an aura of healthy attraction, the attraction of the primitive, of one who lets himself go with the river's current and is happy. Javi pulled him along like a deep-swelling wave, and he had the sensation (when they were wrestling or doing press-ups and seeing the wetness of sweat and agility of muscle) that they had lived a long time together: pirates fighting on foreign seas, soldiers at night, warmed by the flames of friendship, polishing their shields.

Such pirates and soldiers are part of the stock of the homoerotic tradition.[6] They serve Villena as references out to liberatingly contradictory versions of desire, as we have been seeing: the warrior Gonzalo, dissident corsairs in yellow gloves, the subversively self-conscious treatment of the pirate theme in 'El joven de los pendientes de plata' ('The Youth With the Silver Earrings') (*Lugar extraño*, pp.63–4). Within Álvaro's sphere of textual influence though they are restrictive: during the time of the relationship with Javier he writes a 'book of hard, solid prose, like

6. See Dyer, *Now You See It*, pp.47–101 (on Cocteau, Genet and sailors) and pp.111–29 (on soldiers and sailors in the iconography of 1940s underground cultures and in the films of Kenneth Anger); also Woods, *Articulate Flesh*, pp.51–80.

lines of marble,' a set of 'dry' descriptions of the male form 'as if a film-maker had taken a set of very dramatic close-up shots of a single part of the body' (p.105). Although the effect of this book – called *Descanso unidos* (*Together At Rest*) – is, for Carlos, intensely and violently poetic, the close focus can be read as emblematic. Not only does this relationship shut out Carlos and a third close friend María, it frames, belittles and does metaphorical violence to women. Just as the two men abhor femininity in their mutual adoration, so they need excessively to make contact through female sexual companions. The first foursome of the episode is followed by much habitual heterosexual promiscuity and soon by the two men having sex alone – 'it's useless to apply a homosexual pattern, since the story did not allow the name, even though homosexuality it was' (p.101). Thereafter all their exploits are referred back to their closed but still not gay-defined friendship. Just as Sedgwick's theory of homosociality suggests, 'men's "heterosexual desire" for women serves as a more or less perfunctory detour on the way to a close but homophobically proscribed bonding with another man' (quoted in Dollimore, *Sexual Dissidence*, p.157n). So, after some days camping in the pine trees behind a beach on the coast of Almería, days and nights of sex with women and a night of mutual masturbation between themselves, as they return to Madrid Álvaro remembers (musing on his feelings for Javier):

> Las luchas, el esfuerzo (las carreras desnudas que hacían en la playa), la cercanía corporal, la tensión de sentirse iguales, las chicas que dominaban, su apostar por dejarlas exhaustas, mirarse, gustarse a sí mismos, sentir que en el agotamiento hay un abrazo. (p.104)

> The tussles, the physical effort (sprint-racing nude along the beach), the closeness of their bodies, the tension in feeling as equals, the girls they dominated, challenging each other to leave them quite spent, watching each other, taking pleasure in each other, feeling that exhaustion brings with it an embrace.

What Dollimore is able to see in the 'man-man-woman triangle' in renaissance drama is still with us in the late twentieth century: 'the desire which bonds men over women is as erotically invested for the men in relation to each other as for each of them in relation to the woman' (*Sexual Dissidence*, p.304).[7]

---

7. See also *Sexual Dissidence*, pp.157–62 (on Othello and Iago), and pp.304–6 on 'The Erotics Of Masculine Jealousy'.

The next chapter, although narrated by the ever resentful and often misogynistic Carlos, has a quite different sexual political bearing based around its positive representation of the committed feminist and leftist Alma Quesada. She has enormous intellectual resource, charisma, and a keen sense of resistance to the abuses of power. Knowing about men, she eschews close relationships with them because 'she hate[s] tenderness, perhaps because those little affectionate touches are the very framework for the man's domination of the woman' (p.110). She is radical in her politics, siding with what the quietly reactionary Carlos calls extremists and terrorists, and once herself an activist (p.116). She also has a refreshing line on the literary establishment in which Álvaro's new book is involving him: 'Alma told him they had all sold out to Power [...] Álvaro didn't deny it' (pp.114–15). Because she too, from the left-wing politics, brings 'fire and a refusal to conform' (p.110) which is quickly recognised by Álvaro, he gravitates to her, which throws the previous episode with Javier into high (or, indeed, low) relief. Intimacy with men, books about men promoted by men, supposedly apolitical idylls of muscular primitivism, all from this vantage point look questionable from within as well as outside the text.

Alma, the politically beautiful, is however also one of the rebellious damned and leads Álvaro into a heroin habit and closer to the nihilism which ends his story; nevertheless, her active presence, placing Álvaro as it does on the bisexual cusp, is a microtransgression in textual terms which guarantees the dissidence of its gloriously declining hero.

Evading Sexuality

In 'Peter', the narrator's rejection of conventional political opposition and his quest for 'experience' (see Chapter One) is undermined though also perversely strengthened by its association with the adoration of the male body and exaltation of male bonding. The 'very different course' (p.19) his two close buddies take (in going out with women in Madrid) causes the narrator a troubled review of his position as a subject within the political processes of 1968 (eschewing the 'flaming red banners of social action' and favouring 'something more subtle, a more inward, darker, more disturbing and exciting route': p.14):

Mientras hablaba con alguna amiga me fijaba en el torso de un muchacho que otro día – en el autobús – me había contado que jugaba a baloncesto los domingos. Sabía que lo deseaba y que me hubiera gustado ser – de una manera que no habría podido explicarle – su amigo. ¿Cómo decirle que me hubiese encantado haber ido al gimnasio juntos? ¿Cómo afirmarle que su grata virilidad era mi desasosiego y mi reposo? No, yo no era un *marica* [...] buscaba un sendero que no concluía de hallar, una pista que olía a noche, a quimera, a sexo, a ruptura. Silenciosamente lo llamaba *experiencia*. (p.14)

Talking to a girlfriend I would always be thinking of the torso of a boy who a couple of days before – on the bus – had told me how he played basketball every Sunday. I knew that I desired him and that I would have liked to have been – in some way that I would not have been able to explain – his friend. How could I tell him that I would have loved to go to the gym with him? How assure him that his gracious virility was my anxiety and my repose? No, I was not a *queer* [...] I was looking for a path which I had not yet been able to find, which smelt of the night, of strange dreams, of sex, of breaking out. Silently I called it *experience*.

This, as is usually the case with incomplete comings-out, grasps still at caveats like straws (I'm not exactly gay, I just happen to like men's bodies). As is usually the case with this narrator, coalescence into fixed categories is avoided along with stylistically normalised prose (the fast-switching register here is characteristically unsettling). Abandoned also is any sense of wanting to reproduce 'ordinary' relationships: how indeed assure a young jock of such a thing without meeting with ridicule and incomprehension? The narrator's insecurity is increasingly revealed as he recounts how Peter and Jose frequent 'certain American-style bars', drawn to them only by their interest in 'mere sex', and seek out 'English and American girls [...] [who are] much more *liberated* and naturally disposed to pleasure than Spanish girls' (p.19). This 'naturally disposed' shows a complex mix of heterophobia, misogyny and lack of liberation from the myths and mind-set of machismo in the late Franco era, and it is in this immediate narrative and sexual-political context that the eighteen-year-old narrator meets Susan:

A mí Susan (que tendría unos veintiséis años y había estado ya casada) me parecía muy mayor, y sumamente lejana a mi ideal de belleza. Creí sentir, además, que me miraba con cierto recelo, aunque la cosa, a lo mejor, no pasaba de extrañeza. [...] Yo era *raro* para ella (quizá también sospechaba) y ella a mí me resultaba antipática e intrusa porque destruía con su presencia de *vieja* el círculo masculino que era mío. (pp.19–20)

To me, Susan (who must have been about twenty-six and had already been married once) seemed very old and very far indeed from my ideal of beauty. I thought I sensed that she looked at me with a certain amount of mistrust, although perhaps it was just a question of her thinking I was strange, no more than that. [...] I was an *oddity* in her eyes (and perhaps she had guessed about me too) and to me she seemed disagreeable, and an intrusion, because by being there and being *the older woman* she destroyed the circle of male companionship which I considered mine.

With sexism, ageism, and bodyism added to his discourse, the narrator is constructed as unpoliticised, sexually naive, closet homosexual male projecting his own complexes into a suspicion of Woman (as Other) which he then transfers to the woman who happens to be in his vicinity.

As the story progresses, Peter's sex with women becomes one of a triad of factors which lead to his eventual breakdown and institutionalisation as a hopeless case in a psychiatric hospital in Canada. It is linked, strongly, to drug-use and to a hybrid counter-cultural lifestyle made up of the decadentism, literature, rock and hippyism which the narrator reads as 'without direction' (see Chapter One above). The strong suggestion is – and it surfaces again in the narrating Carlos in *Beyond the World* – that engagement by men in non-same-sex sex, while theoretically guaranteeing salvation from orthodox sexualities, sabotages the quest for the authentic experience on the edge. Or, put another way, women are a threat to homosociality: and this is the way it is put in the narrative structure of *Beyond the World* where Álvaro is taken from his friends by a series of women and finally by 'la Muerte', by Death as female figure.

We can read on past this scenario of threat and sabotage, though, to see that some women are vital and conversely all gay-identified men dangerous to eroticised homosociality between men in Villena's writing. In 'Rafael' the term 'homosexual' is evaded, nobody is gay as such, male bisexuality is rewritten as a charming and quite usual trait of otherwise straight youth and (in reproduction of common prejudice) as a front. Alternative sexual politics within heterosexuality is represented as an absurd and shaming obstacle to the transgressive project. 'I never liked the

term "homosexual", and still don't', says the narrator in relation
to his 'comradeship' with Rafael in the story of that name (*Chicos*,
pp. 42–71, p.58). It is a remark that places the text on the line
between dissident refusal to succumb to controlling classification
and an evasiveness which traces an act of sexual-political bad faith
which comes from male bonding.

Rafael is the (musical) younger brother of Víctor, with whom the
narrator had struck up a close friendship as a student 'because of
a sudden, fleeting, evasive remark made about a biography of
Oscar Wilde' (p.43) and a certain ambiguity. Víctor lets him down,
though – as in a different way will Rafael – by falling for a
straightforward sexual option and a lifestyle endorsed by straight
culture. His – and later Rafael's – conventional notions of sexuality
are pitilessly marked by one of Villena's stylistic idiosyncracies, the
use of italics. This variously can denote dialogue, hearsay and
speech reported but with a disdainful twist (as in 'Peter' with the
terms *experience, oddity, queer, liberated,* and *older woman*). Thus
Víctor's increasingly conventional homosexuality becomes faintly
ridiculous and certainly restricting. Returning from studying
Chinese in Taiwan (and sleeping with effeminate boys and with
women) Víctor comes to terms with his homosexuality, asks the
narrator to give him an entry onto the gay scene, then, opting for
the world of steady relationships, asks him to live with him (which
the narrator turns down). He then settles for a fifty-year-old
American soldier from the base at Torrejón, eventually going off
with him to the USA. Both the fact that after Taiwan 'he never
mentioned the word *bisexuality* again' and that 'he wanted *a man*'
are marked off, in those italics, as a threat to true dissidence and
to the narrator's decorum: '*a man*, he used that very word, one
which to me was quite extraordinary and almost monstrous' (pp.56
and 60). Worse still, one of the things which prevents the narrator
from consummating his budding 'comradeship' with Rafael is the
thought of Víctor's being 'more and more at ease with his own
homosexuality but inflexibly condemning of what, restrictively, he
called *pederasty*, and anyway so severe about anything concerning
his younger brother (p.59).

Víctor's desire for a 'masculine happiness' (p.57) and for the
obligatory 'simplicity' of happiness, as well as his prudishness,
creates a rupture which is matched in Rafael's drift towards a non-
same-sex sex relationship with Isabel who is framed thus:

Ojos grandes, cejas oscuras, algo de acné – esas chicas jamás usaban maquillaje – y no muy guapa. Era simpática, muy desenvuelta [...] dispuesta naturalmente a adelantar terreno, a conquistárselo, con apariencia afable, a quien tuviera enfrente. ¿Me caía antipática – debo decir la palabra – por eso? ¿Por su aire de *progre liberada* y muy activa? ¿O eran celos porque – no sé si puedo decirlo – me había quitado a Rafael, con quien yo me había portado siempre tan al revés que ella, con tanto apocamiento? (pp.66–7)

Large eyes, dark eyebrows, a bit of acne – these girls never use make-up – and not very attractive. She was easy to get on with, very laid back [...] with a natural tendency to gain ground, to take advantage of whoever came her way while still appearing affable. Is that why, as I must say, I did not like her at all? Because of her *trendy, liberated* and very outgoing ways? Or was it jealousy – I don't know if I can bear to say this – because she had taken Rafael away from me, Rafael with whom my behaviour had always been so different from her own, so very timid?

The use of the word *progre* (trendy, with overtones of belated hippyism) amounts to a class judgement, aligning the narrator (not for the first time) with that group for whom to be 'progressive' is to be vulgar. There is alignment too with a certain gay misogynistic viewpoint which codes colourful dress and assertiveness in women also as vulgar, as a sign of the superiority of the likes of the delicate Rafael. The narrative is beginning to reveal the pressures being brought to bear by the multiplicity of conflicting histories of transgression which are its dynamic.

The last meeting between the narrator and Rafael, like the first, has as its pretext a book – on medieval music, minstrels and troubadours for a study the narrator is writing – thus aligning him with Arturo in *Amour Passion* in hyper-cultural self-delusion. Rafael (now nineteen) meets him with the book, they go to a café but there is none of the previous intimacy between them: Rafael is coarse, callow and brusque, and they are soon joined there by Isabel (pp.64–71). After a drink Rafael asks straight out if he and Isabel can come back and use the narrator's flat to have sex. He wretchedly agrees to this and gets sucked into a nightmare of embarrassment, seeing his own expectation of sophisticated behaviour once they are all back home as foolishness: 'If we'd already spoken, and if we knew that we were not going back to the house just for this, then why quite, for the sake of what absurd ceremony need we go through with the pretence of a drawing-room drama?' (p.68). Looking back, he is unable, and unwilling, to remember clearly the sequence of his actions or the motivation of his behaviour. The whole incident is contorted with shame and revelation. Hearing them come out of the shower he goes to the room, 'Perhaps to tell them not to bother with tidying up after them (I imagined them with freshly combed hair, putting the bed straight) perhaps as a friendly gesture of trust' (p.69). Both the banal domestic politeness and that strait-laced supposition bring our usually sophisticated narrator down low; and as for his otherwise well-honed sensitivities in matters of companionship, they fail him badly. He stumbles on the couple having sex again and creates a tableau which has the double power of being faintly unappetising and aesthetically arresting:

> Entré, tratando de resultar simpático, y les hallé sobre la cama desnudos, retorcidos y besándose. ¿No habían podido contener un nuevo arrebato erótico? ¿O se trataba de una provocación, según mi sospecha? Parecieron no enterarse de mi llegada, y vi el blanco cuerpo largo de Rafael frotándose ardorosamente sobre el bastante más oscuro de su amiga. Oí el frú-frú de la saliva en sus labios. Observé la dulce juventud de sus miembros. Creo que me quedé extático, paralizado. Y de repente parecieron darse cuenta de que yo estaba allí [...] Isabel hizo un gesto (no concluso) de llevarse una mano, como una hoja de parra, al pubis. Rafael no hizo el menor ademán por ocultar su miembro, casi plenamente erecto. (p.69)

> I went in, trying to be friendly, and I found them on the bed entwined, naked and kissing. Had they been unable to resist the onset of another bout of erotic activity? Or was this meant as provocation, as I suspected then? They seemed not to notice my arrival, and I saw Rafael's long white body rubbing hotly against his girlfriend's considerably darker skin. I heard the slurping of saliva on their lips. I saw the soft youthfulness of their limbs. I think I stood there ecstatic, paralysed. And then suddenly they seemed to notice I was there [...] Isabel made a move (but stopped half way) to place her hand, like a vine-leaf, over her pubis. Rafael made not the slightest movement to hide his now almost fully erect member.

Rafael's excitement, had it been directed towards what has been coded by the text as angelic love, should have been the first step on the ladder to a pure eternal beauty; instead it stands as a crass and brutal sign of change and ugly impossibility. This blunt heterosexual scene framed in a doorway roughly erases the high artistic aspirations and idealisations inscribed in Rafael's name.

Twice during this episode comes the painful realisation that Rafael has changed. The first is in retrospect, when the narrator is wondering what he had felt while sitting there before in the drawing-room waiting: 'Jealousy again? The desire to go and spy on them, or strain to hear their panting through the door? No, it wasn't that, although envy and the lowest of appetites may well have played their part. Above all what I felt was confusion and wretchedness' (p.68). Here the perception of the change in Rafael is prompted by at least a half-recognition of the sordid and profane. The second incident of painful realisation comes a page later, after the bedroom scene, and in the presence of the after-image of Rafael's erection:

> Volvieron a sonreír y comenzaron a ponerse la ropa interior. ¿Hablamos más? ¿Acepté su ritual agradecimiento casi mudo? ¿Les acompañé al umbral prometiendo o sugiriendo que volviésemos a vernos? Es posible, pero no tenía sentido. Rafael – que probablemente quiso burlarse de mí, decirme que me había equivocado – no era el que yo había conocido, coqueteado y soñado parsimoniosamente. Era otro. Y a ella – *progre* de pelo hirsuto – la odiaba. (p.69)

> They smiled again and started to put on their underwear. Did we say anything else? Did I just accept their ritual thanks almost in silence? Did I accompany them to the door with a promise that we would meet again, or suggesting we should? Possibly, but there was no sense in it. Rafael – who probably had done this to mock me, tell me I had been mistaken – was no longer the Rafael I had so tentatively known, flirted with and dreamt about. He was another person. And as for her – with her long hair and progressive ways – I hated her.

Again there is an instability at the source of the story and at the point of its telling: the narrator is neither sure now of what he did nor was he certain then of the Rafael he thought he knew. Whereas the ecstasy is linked, though the phrase 'youthful limbs' and the colour white, to high art, statuary and classical perfection (linked, that is, to the Rafael of memory and to a certain homosexual culture), the paralysis which is its pair is due to the presence in the house of heterosexuality, of the girl with long hair, an unclassical colouring and progressive ways who is represented as the dual demon of shame and non-same-sex sex. The bond between the narrator and Rafael, between the present and the past is broken. Isabel has even changed – vulgarised Rafael's name, 'She was studying music too, like *Rafa*, she called him' (p.66). Rafael might be an archangel's name, but Rafa evokes the banal scenes and habits of late teenage life rather than angels in Italian paintings. The story begins by making Rafael an icon: 'It is an archangel's name, and it might remind the more aesthetically inclined of an Italian painting' (p.41). It ends with him dealing an all too human slap in the face. The noise of that slap, delivered by non-same-sex sex in the guise of a bisexuality which is painfully not identical with its term, echoes back to the early part of the story.

> [Rafael] optó por lo que era su mayor preferencia. Pero en realidad Rafael representa a miles, a casi todos los muchachos. Y la bisexualidad – una máscara para mí y para cuantos pudorosamente la necesitaron – resulta a la postre cierta. Y entonces Rafael – el *Rafa* de su amiga – se acerca retrospectivamente a Víctor y a mí (que simbolizamos la natural, obtusa ceguera de nuestro tiempo joven) y con una sonrisa sardónica y cargada de ironía, fingiéndose algo bufón y pirado, nos da un leve pero eficaz cachete en la cara. Un bofetón que suena. Y se va. Y nos quedamos solos. (pp.70–1)

> Rafael [...] opted for what was his first preference. But really [he] represents thousands, almost all boys. And bisexuality – a mask for me and for all whose sense of shame makes them feel they need one – turns out in the end to be true. And so the figure of Rafael – or '*Rafa*' as his girlfriend calls him – comes up, retrospectively, towards me and Victor (symbolising as we do the natural, obtuse blindness of our younger days) and with a sardonic smile, heavy with irony, pretending to play the fool and skipping about, he slaps us lightly but effectively in the face. The sound of the blow rings out. And then he goes. And we are left alone.

The angel has abandoned them and a shifting sexuality, which should be a liberation, turns out to be a multi-positioned trap, turning out both to be 'true' and not true.

Rafael's sleeping with a woman (like Peter in his story) breaks the delicate (illusory) equilibrium of relations of desire required for the ideal but eroticised friendship. In another direction though this shift of behaviour and desire can be a key to the construction of that comradeship by way of the classic buddy narrative where women as adventure and object of sex-talk bring the guys closer. Thus the ghastly Claudio Goli in the story 'Gonzalo' arrogantly takes bisexuality for granted and is given to asking boys ironically 'so have you left that girl yet?' ('¿Has dejado ya a la chavala?': p.163); while in the story 'Juan-José' (pp.127–55), Santi comes to the narrator's body via an understanding woman's bed. The collapsing structures in this story are again triangular. The narrator is going out at first with refined but frigid Juan-José, 'pale and archangelic, serious and absorbed' with 'fine, classical looks, with a hint of the statuesque about him, but more subtle and pre-Raphaelite' (pp.129 and 131), but he really desires the more raunchy and uncomplicated Santi. Santi's desires are heterosexually identified but he also has a strong desire for good times which for him are located in a scene and lifestyle where if boys admire women they also admire and love each other and are coveted by men. Santi is drawn by this and by the narrator's obsessive interest. Santi – unlike Juan-José in his sober shirts and jackets and lace-up shoes – is first seen in what seems to be an XL-size American football shirt with a Wyoming State logo, and he is typified by it: 'we called him "Wyo"' (p.143). He is sixteen, a frequenter of the wildest and most exclusive disco, Mercurio, and an energetic dancer:

> Parecía un muchachito californiano de aquellos que practicaban el monopatín por las cuestas de San Francisco, todos color de playa. Era guapo y el rostro resultaba suave, añinado y viril. Y el cuerpo, esbelto y grácil, era a la par fuerte y duro: Capitán del equipo de *hockey* en el colegio en que acababa sus estudios. Resultaba ingenuo, pero también apasionado, cálido, deseoso de mundo, hambriento, jubiloso como el amanecer, afanoso por semejar liberado, cabalgador y moviéndose en realidad, airada y hermosamente para romper las ataduras. [...] Jamás hablaba de arte ni de libros. Había hecho de su alma (preciosa y azul) un cuerpo perfecto. (p.144)

> He looked like a California teenager, one of those boys who skateboard on the hills of San Francisco, all of them beach-blond. He was handsome, and his face looked soft, boyish and virile all at once. And his body, though slim and graceful, was hard and strong too: the captain of his hockey team [...] He came across as ingenuous, but also warm, full of enthusiasm and with a desire to see life, hungry for experience, joyful as the dawn, keen to show that he was free and galloping wild and beautiful, really moving, shaking off the traces. [...] He never talked about art or books. He had transformed his soul (his precious, blue soul) into a perfect body.

Refusing to reside entirely in either of the realms of body or of 'soul', he represents the perfect idol for Villena's equivocal cult of evasion and pursuit of the ideal. After a night in Mercurio, Marta (a Brazilian of German origins, about twenty-five, and exotically aware of her attractiveness) invites the narrator, Enrique (another friend) and Santi back to her flat. Santi is fascinated by her (perhaps

not least because 'she served the drinks *topless*') and by the whole
atmosphere ('on the brink of dawn, finishing the last of many
drinks, amid excess and barbiturates': pp.145 and 146). The
narrator says of Marta that 'she always used to say all good-looking
boys – *really* good-looking, she would insist – end up going to bed,
sooner rather than later, with other boys' (p.145). Having got Santi
into the bedroom with her, and excited, she refuses to have sex with
him on the grounds that he has never had sex with another man.

Two common gay popular myths are being invoked here: the
wishful belief about handsome and mostly straight boys which is
put into Marta's mouth; and, in a version of the dynamics of
homosociality, the myth of the understanding woman as facilitating
blank space, either as a cipher through which homoerotic bonding
may be processed and consummated, or as the younger gay man's
chaperone and *animateuse* on the scene. The second is more
problematic and more internalized by the text and centres on the
proposition, in Villena's versions, that contact by boys with
attractive women can act as a catalyst to their desirability. In 'Juan'
the young women and the boys strike sparks off one another's
beauty in the disco El Sultán and the women are there as protectors
and accessories to the boys (a set-up by no means confined to
Villena's Madrid): 'Many of the boys there were clearly
homosexual, although they always liked to be seen with slim,
blonde girlfriends' (p.18). Similarly, the presence of women (who,
perhaps needless to say, must be glamorous) can lead to a kind of
wry and pleased awareness in the narrator and other male
onlookers of the way they complement the desirability of the boys.
In a disco like Mercurio in 'Juan José' beautiful young women are
part and parcel of the delightfulness of 'that exquisite, carefree,
lovely micro-world' (p.143) and the mysterious Marta rules over
a glittering world of bisexuality which leads to the narrator's
getting Santi for himself for a while. But it leads also, with the
arrival of Santi's English girlfriend Mabel, to the end of glamour.
This aspect of bisexuality is a nuisance: 'Santi was leaving our
gilded Dorian fields and was returning to the everyday world'
(p.152).

On other occasions cross-gender contact will incur a rather
sharper treatment, as in 'Rafael' and 'Peter'. The fate meted out to
Juan (in the story of that name: pp.183–205) is of a different nature,
but more telling, for he is sent into the limbo of marriage and a
conventional life, explicitly echoing (on p.205) Wilde's regret about

'the enormous number of young men [...] who start life with perfect profiles, and end by adopting some useful profession.'[8] He is, at the start of the story, a delicately beautiful boy whom the narrator fails to seduce and he is described as having in him 'a propensity for debauchery ('un tirón *vicioso*'), a certain appetite for the exceptional and the depraved, and a *nostalgie de la boue* no doubt typical in one so ethereal, so fragile and so angelic' (p.192). This urge leads him into an emotionally masochistic relationship in a triangle with the narrator and Eduardo, an aggressively sexy lad with a punk sensibility whose charms are described as being a 'whip' to Juan's desire for a long-term relationship (p.192) but who is more interested in the narrator (himself increasingly in love with Juan). Although Juan has vanilla sex with the narrator (once), his interests shift, first to heavy sex with Gonzalo, then to cutting the narrator direct one night and then away from them all to camp teenagers in 'rather sordid bars or late-night cellar-clubs' whom he takes outside for casual sex in alleyways (p.204). The final stop on his descent, as the narrator is able to observe one day years later, is boring married life with 'an enchanting little blonde [...] an over-dainty little wife' ('una mujercita dengosa') and life with two noisy kids (p.205). The tacit equation of marriage with morbid perversion and the fall from grace is as forceful and radical as it is unfair and misogynistic.

Even harsher treatment comes in 'Emilio' (pp.101–25). When the narrator says of Emilio 'I knew about [his] adventures on the female side, but they are never an obstacle' (p.117) there is a minor narratorial spitefulness to come (as the disdainful brushing aside of such 'adventures' already suggests). In the story's final paragraph he remembers that he thought he saw Emilio's name on a poster advertising a light comedy, '*Wicked Weeks*, or something like that' (p.126), and this is an observation which gains in tartness when we recall an earlier, theatrical light S/M scene between Emilio and the narrator with a leather belt (pp.115–17) which had then been sexy, but now is downgraded to mere arch daring by association with the sleazy show. The narrator does not let up: 'I saw him appear afterwards – in very secondary roles – in a couple of undistinguished films' (p.126). Into the atmosphere of this paragraph come two wry suggestions about Emilio's fate: 'Perhaps

8. In 'Phrases and Philosophies for the Use of the Young', Wilde, *Complete Works*, p.1, 203.

{ 106 }

he has become a Civil Guard he once dreamed of being. Perhaps he is being kept by an older woman' (p.126).

The women who are vital to the right sort of bonding are women like the 'Woman of the World' (see Chapter One), elegant, outside conventional sexual politics and admired, but paying the price of textual marginalisation. Alma Quesada, Isabel and even Marta, on the other hand, are to differing degrees resented by the narrating voices because they have a more central role in the text and have real access to the progressive and the transgressive. Above all they can control men's bodies and desires: they are women who, uncomfortably for the narrators, write History back into desire, they are proactive, making their dissidence live through an era of transition and not projecting it onto an ideal realm of no fixed cultural abode. Mabel, Emilio's older woman, and Sixto's and Juanjo's eventual partners are emblems of the fall into dull conformity. All these women challenge the idealistic cult of high homosociality in their diverse ways but they also highlight difference and reveal the fissures in the monolith of conventional sexuality.

'Gonzalo': False Consciousness

The homosocial dream which is both criticised and exalted in so many of the stories is, as much as an idealisation, a partly ironic dramatisation. From certain perspectives male bonding is seen as bringing with it a blatant inauthenticity in the narrating subject. It may lead to excessive coding of relationships (as with Arturo), to an intermittently reactionary sexual politics (as in *Boys*), or to recognised betrayals of ethical principles by Villena as author.

A link between narrator, love and theatricality is established in 'Juan José' which represents some of these dangers. One night in another disco, Mercurio, the narrator is challenged by his friend Enrique as to why he has abandoned the elegant, cultivated and beautiful Juan José (or Juanjo) for the raunchier and much more uncomplicated Santi (although he is still in love with Juanjo):

> yo (ya estimulado por el *whisky*) le dije en voz alta: *Querido, nosotros los refinados queremos lo primitivo*. Y empecé a repetirlo muchas veces, traduciéndolo al francés y con mucho teatro. Juanjo me oía, intuyendo quizá que me refería a él, pero sin darse por aludido. En ese momento amaba de veras. Y amar (no podemos olvidarlo) es un don y también un martirio. Por ello el enamorado – el amante genuino – es luego

capaz de odio. [...] La frasecita aquella [...] la lanzaba yo contra Juanjo
– ebrio del otro – como azotándole con una fusta pequeña. (pp.148–9)

I said to him (enlivened now by the whisky) loudly: 'But my dear, we
refined souls always love the primitive.' And I began to repeat it over
and over, translating it into French and being very dramatic. Juanjo
heard me, perhaps thinking that I was referring to him, but pretending
not to hear. At that moment I was truly in love. And love (we should
never forget) is a gift and also a martyrdom . . . That is why the genuine
lover – the one who is really in love – is so capable of hatred. [...] I meant
that little phrase for Juanjo – dazzled as I was by the other – as if I were
using it as a tiny whip with which to beat him.

There is an instability here that goes beyond mere self-awareness
on the part of the narrator. This scene signals uncertainty as to the
status of such apothems as 'And love (we should never forget) is a
gift and also a martyrdom': for all that it is coded with wisdom and
necessary for the justification of the whole scene, it is allowed to
teeter on the brink of the same collapse into absurdity or shame as
afflicts other elaborate adventures of the narrator's. The clumsy
foolishness of alcoholic drunkenness is on the same stage, at the
same level, as the bedazzlement of infatuation (the Spanish
adjective 'ebrio' used by Villena can cover the range from alcoholic
to emotional highs). Spotlighting the squiffy queeniness of the *bons
mots* turns out to be a self-revealing joke at the narrator's – and
Villena's – own expense, but also in their favour, since rather than
forgiving them anything as simple as snobbery we read again here
the double and conflictive flirtation with the excesses of refinement
and the call of the primitive which both enlivens and makes
politically perverse so many of the scenes and texts they set up. Sex
sends shimmers of uncertainty through the whole textual network.

Gonzalo, in his story, is one of the most dubious of the characters
in *Boys* and it is a challenge to know how to read him. His
association with Claudio Goli – a showy aristocrat, lifelong
supporter of Franco and sympathiser with the far right – put him
at a considerable distance from the counter-cultural ideal. The
narrator's meeting with Gonzalo earlier on that first night of sex
prompts an awkward interruption of the personal history by
political and social history:

[Gonzalo] me dio el punto de cita: La puerta de *California-47*. Un lugar
para ir a otro. Eran los días previos a las primeras elecciones
democráticas, tras la muerte del dictador: Fines de mayo de 1977. Un

país en ebullición, vitalísimo, contradictorio, fantástico, lleno de presagios negros, pero también – y más – de un inmenso apetito de aurora. La ciudad estaba llena de carteles y pintadas diversas, provocadoras, libérrimas. Y en la puerta de *California-47*, aquel preámbulo nocturno, estaba instalada una gran mesa, con propaganda y símbolos de *Fuerza Nueva*. La custodiaban dos muchachos vestidos con camiseta azul y boina roja, aguiluchos facistas, llenos de orgullo, apostura, y teatralidad macabra. A quienes no sentíamos así, todo aquel aparato paramilitar – por qué no decirlo – nos daba miedo, nos imponía. Lo que es terrible, pues, es precisamente lo que buscaban: Someter, impresionar. Gonzalo no tardó en llegar. Venía muy hermoso [...] y le dije, en seguida, que nos fuéramos de allí porque era muy incómoda la presencia de aquel escuadrón de *fachas*, dispuestos siempre como están al cabreo y la pendencia. Entonces Gonzalo, sin decir nada, pero acentuando la gelidez mineral de su sonrisa (una sonrisa pequeña y bella) se desabrochó lentamente la chaqueta azul de botones dorados, y vi que la camiseta blanca llevaba un letrero azul también: *Fuerza Nueva*. (pp.164–5)

[Gonzalo] suggested where we should meet: at the door of *California-47*. A place to go on from. It was in the days running up to the first democratic elections, after the death of the dictator: towards the end of May 1977. A country seething with energy, extraordinary vitality, contradictions, fantasies; full of dark omens, but also – and more so – with an immense appetite for the dawn of a new age. The city was full of posters and graffiti, diverse, provocative and incredibly liberated. And at the door of *California-47*, that prefatory night, there was a large table set up with *Fuerza Nueva* propaganda and insignia.[9] Two boys in blue shirts and red berets were in charge of it, two little fascist eaglets, full of pride, smart looks and macabre theatricality. To those of us who did not feel as they did, all this militaristic paraphernalia – why not admit it? – frightened and oppressed us. Which is a terrible thing, since that is exactly what they wanted to do: to dominate and to impress. Gonzalo soon arrived, looking very handsome [...] and I said to him at once that we should move on because it was uncomfortable having that little squad of fascists there, spoiling as always for an argument and a fight. Then Gonzalo, without a word, but intensifying his steely, glacial smile (it was a little smile, and a beautiful one) slowly unbuttoned his blue jacket with its gold buttons, and I saw that his white tee-shirt had a blue logo on it too: *Fuerza Nueva*.

9. *Fuerza Nueva*: an extreme right-wing party under the leadership of Blas Piñar, founder of the neo-Fascist review of the same name.

California-47 then is a place of involved transition, the meeting at its threshold and the first unbuttoning of Gonzalo's clothing mark the commencement of a period of difficult complicity. The narrator's opposition to the aims of the Fuerza Nueva, clear anyway from other stories, is manifest: although Gonzalo soon reveals that he no longer is with Fuerza Nueva, his use of the word *'reds'* (*'rojos'*) and stories of participation in attacks disturb the narrator (pp.166–7). However, just as the parenthetical detail of Gonzalo's smile – '(it was a little smile, and a beautiful one)' – so tellingly interrupts and eroticises the revelation of Gonzalo's affiliation, so too is the probity of the narrator's counter-cultural discourse in *Boys* disrupted by the presence of Gonzalo. In his effort to assimilate Gonzalo into the drama (and get him into bed) the narrator half leaves aside and half accepts the macabre element in this part of the story. He allows himself to play a part dictated by the excitement, the contradictions, the liberating signs of the current political situation, and in doing so he reveals a political incorrectness and a personal instability brought about by the combination of desire for absolute change and desire for absolute male beauty. The Fuerza Nueva logo on Gonzalo's shirt is met with an equivocal laugh and a double take: 'Although I was taken aback (how could I not be), at the same time I had to laugh at my astonishment' (p.165). With a laugh, Gonzalo is problematically reframed. The logo becomes one more in the dynamic array of slogans denoting transition and liberation, a perversely liberating and deliciously provocative costume in the drama. A taste for uniform and Germanic good-looks is interwoven with multiple strands of idolisation and delusion:

> Pensé en *El ocaso de los dioses*. Gonzalo pertenecía a esa camada que busca la perfección del vicio, su hondura, el exquisito privilegio de su diferencia, y al mismo tiempo, tralla y fusta para la grey aplebeyada y miserable. Cóndores reales volando, superhombres y majestuosos, sobre misérrimas y adocenadas ovejas.
>
> Notó mi estupor y se echó a reir también, claramente, mientras comenzamos a andar, sin rumbo, Goya abajo. Yo comencé a excusarme, reteniendo (en mi claudicación) algo de pudor. Dije – torpe, apresuradamente – que nada tenía contra la derecha, nada, aunque sí creía (siendo yo de derechas) que aquello, su violencia, su tremendismo, era exagerado, incivil, innecesario. (pp.165–6)

It brought to mind *The Damned*. Gonzalo belonged to that brood of beings who seek the perfection and depth of vice, the exquisite pleasure of their difference and, at the same time, seek it as a whip and lash for the miserable, plebeian herd. Regal condors, majestic supermen swooping above the poor, wretched, common sheep.

Gonzalo noticed my astonishment and began to laugh too, a loud, clear laugh as we walked, not knowing where we were heading, down Goya. I began to make excuses, without losing (in my backing-down) a certain sense of shame. I said – clumsily and hastily – that I had no objection to the Right, none whatsoever, although I thought (being of the Right myself) that all this, the violence, its brutal, frank presentation, was exaggerated, uncivilised and unnecessary.

This mutual laughter, the aimless wandering and the narrator's unfocused near-blustering words cast some interesting shadows of doubt over this scene, the relationship, the narrator's reliability and – conceivably – Villena's too. Gonzalo's insertion into the frame of Visconti's film and its ethos oils the wheels of the evening and leads to the narrator agreeing to go to the restaurant Korinto – where Gonzalo had seen Orson Welles eat one night – and paying for an expensive and exquisite meal of seafood and Ribeiro wine, in the after-glow of which he decides that:

> Gonzalo no era ya el niño *facha* que había temido. Amaba el elitismo, se creía superior (físicamente lo era) pero la política no le interesaba. Su meta ahora – como en tantos de su edad y de varia condición social – estaba en el placer, en el goce, en el extremado autodeleite de la juventud. Vivir siempre alto, arriba, como los dioses viven. Lo dijo en otras palabras. (pp.167–8)

> Gonzalo was not the fascist youth I had feared. He loved elitism, thought himself superior (and physically he was) but politics did not interest him. His aim now – as with so many of his age of various social conditions – lay in pleasure, enjoyment, the extreme self-delight of youth. To live high up above like the gods live. He himself used different words to say this.

But the narrator's expansion on the Visconti film and his clearly if laconically marked rewriting of what Gonzalo says here prompt continuing reappraisals of the slant we are to take on the tale and its teller, even if towards the protagonist (being distant from his sexual charms) feelings might be less uncertain. On the one hand the narrator is revealed as writing over the top, and rewriting Gonzalo ('He himself used different words'). On the other, Gonzalo is effectively elevated for the narrator, saved from the crassness of impressionable and inarticulate youth as well as that of direct political involvement.

Beyond his association in the narrator's mind with *The Damned* and his own desire to be associated, albeit at a snobbish tangent, with Orson Welles, Gonzalo is in fact already implicated at this stage in the story in a cinematic fantasy which in turn has implicated the narrator and elevates the two of them, only then to tip them into absurdity by way of excess. When the narrator turns up at the discothèque *Love* one night late in 1976 – not yet having heard of Gonzalo – he is greeted by a friend Gustavo, who is 'completely gone, euphoric, sparks flying from his eyes, as if he had just witnessed a miracle' (p.158), and who greets him with the craftily dramatic words 'he's just left, you'll never see him now, he's just this minute gone out through the door' (p.158). 'He' is Gonzalo, whose very absence blesses the scene with angelic light so that the coming story is already framed in such a way that the narrator will be the wonder-struck mortal lifted for a time from the sorry floor of the world. However, when Gonzalo returns to the disco shortly afterwards and the narrator's gaze is turned his way it is the boy who is rendered all image, art and object to be not only lifted up but set at a distance as ironic as it is admiring:

> Gustavo, apenas verlo, corrió a hacerle zalemas. De haber tenido una legión de chinos, con túnicas de dragones, les habría puesto en fila, con un farolito, para escoltar la entrada de Gonzalo, Príncipe imperial. Reconozco que me acerqué con cautela y casi antipatía. Debo reconocer también que – ya de cerca – me tocó la luz, me derribó el aura del prodigio. ¿Por qué no? Gonzalo parecía exactamente eso: Un ser de otro mundo. Alguien (lo pensé) no nacido para la tierra. Quizá el habitante de otra galaxia estética. Una lujosa Andrómeda. Aunque es difícil – he visto muchos – estoy por decir que Gonzalo era el muchacho más guapo, más perfectamente bello que hubiera visto nunca. (p.158)

> scarcely had he seen him than Gustavo ran over to pay him homage. If he had had at his disposal a legion of Chinese soldiers with dragon-embroidered tunics he would have drawn them up into a column, with a lantern before them, to escort Gonzalo, an Imperial Prince, on his entrance. I admit I felt a certain reticence, even dislike, as I went over. I also have to admit that – close to – the light reached out and touched me, and I was struck by the aura surrounding this prodigy. And why not? Gonzalo seemed to be just that, a being from another world. Someone not born (I remember thinking) to live on this earth. Perhaps the inhabitant of an altogether different aesthetic galaxy. Some

luxurious Andromeda. Although it's difficult – I've seen so many – I would say that Gonzalo was, just there and then, the most handsome, most perfectly beautiful boy I had ever seen.

The narrator's 'And why not?' signals his awareness of the stylistic risks of such a theatrical presentation. It does not, though, only ask that we indulge him on the detail of Gonzalo's extra-terrestrial loveliness but also points to a further, unrecognised excess: the camp, operatic fantasy imputed to Gustavo so amusingly is of course only displaced from the narrator himself. The worldly 'I've seen so many' notwithstanding, the narrator is bewitched (and, at the time narrated, fairly drunk) (p.159). Coded with Apollonian beauty, Gonzalo is set against the deliquescence of luxurious detail: a geometrically perfect face, very blue eyes, lightly golden skin, 'following the Germanic model Visconti favoured as the ideal effigy of aristocratic values' (p.159), a hard, handsome air about him with that icy smile. Outrageously – 'with grandiloquent, sweeping gestures, abetted by the rings worn artistically on my fingers [...] full of theatricality and self-confidence' (p.159) – the narrator suggests (loudly) to him that he star in a short film he is thinking of making about the young emperor Heliogabalus.

> un *corto*, que resultaría muy especial: Nuevo cine poético [...] La fugaz, intensa y loca historia del césar Heliogábalo – que no hacía mucho había leído – me trajo una imagen fascinadora: la de un adolescente guapo y todopoderoso, entregado al placer y a la perfección de la vida. Existía, sobre todo, un instante deslumbrador – y ése iba a ser el cenit de mi *corto* – : asediado por las tropas de Macrino que vienen a destruirlo, Heliogábalo sube a la torre de su fortaleza en Siria (yo filmaría, simplificándolo, un torreón en la llanura un día soleado) y allí, en su cúspide se desnuda bajo la luz, como asumiéndola o encarnándola – al astro vivo – y las legiones se detienen y deponen los escudos, porque la dorada belleza de aquel muchacho (su melena al viento, y el viento acariciando, enamorado, su piel melada) les fulmina como la aparición de un ser superior, trastornador, perfecto. El dios en su parusía. Como el ángel (no se lo dije) que semejaba Gonzalo. Por eso era él mi emperador – que borrachera tan dulce la de aquella noche – y mi protagonista. (pp.159–60)

> a short, which in my mind was going to be very special indeed: the New Poetic Cinema. [...] The brief, intense and crazy story of the caesar Heliogabalus – which I had not long ago read – brought to my mind a fascinating image: that of a handsome and all-powerful adolescent

boy, given over to pleasure and to the perfection of life. There was, above all – and this was to be the zenith of my short – a dazzling moment: under siege from the troops of Macrinus who are coming to destroy him, Heliogabalus goes up into the tower of his Syrian fortress (which I would simplify by filming on a castle turret somewhere out on the Castilian plain on a sunny day) and there, at the pinnacle, he strips naked in the sunlight, taking it to him or incarnating it – the living star – and the legions stop still and put down their shields because the beauty of the boy (his long hair flying on the wind, and the wind, enraptured, caressing his honeyed skin) strikes them as the blazing apparition of a superior, disturbing and perfect being. The god at his Second Coming. Like the angel (and I didn't tell him this) which Gonzalo seemed to be. That is why he was my emperor – what sweet drunkenness that night – and my protagonist.

Converted into the object of the narratorial gaze, like so many of the boys and men Villena represents, Gonzalo in the early part of this story becomes almost the victim of a 'violent' representation ('almost' because he is later to be obliquely empowered, and is male), like the represented woman in Teresa de Lauretis' well-known account of narrative cinema's inscription of gender 'fixed in the position of icon, spectacle, or image to be looked at [and bearing] the mobile look of both the spectator and the male character(s)' (*Technologies*, p.44). The adventure Gonzalo represents is the 'other space' of the mythical subject described by de Lauretis in her elaboration of Lotman's theory of plot typology as 'an element of plot-space, a topos, a resistance, matrix and matter' (p.43). Gonzalo appears in iconic stills on other occasions in the story: once at the end of a telephone being evasive about a second meeting; once in sun-glasses sitting up on the rolled-back convertible roof of Goli's Jaguar, hair flying in the wind of a 'luminous winter's day', like (again) 'the young emperor [...], an undefeated adolescent general, about to enter the city in triumph' (*Chicos*, p.162); and lastly, in the disco Time, all dressed in white:

> El negro ambiente y las luces de la pista rebotaban en el blanco y el oro de Gonzalo. Su mirada – dura y bella – fulminaba a todos los pecadores, míseros nacidos de alrededor a quienes echaba de su paraíso con aquella total espada de fuego. ¿Cómo evitar de nuevo las comparación querubínica? Bastaban los ojos. (p.163)

> The black surroundings and the lights on the dance-floor were sent bouncing back off the white and the gold which were Gonzalo. His look – beautiful and severe – struck down all those low-born sinners

round about whom he expelled from his paradise with that flaming
sword of absolute fire. How once again to avoid the angelic
comparison? It was enough to see his eyes.

Despite the dehumanising representations though, Gonzalo is
also partially recast as the adventurer and setter of scenes, more
master than matrix. When he suggests to the narrator, after sex, that
they should go off together 'to Paris or Nice for a week' (pp.168–
9) the narrator is seduced into the subordinate role of provider of
luxury and good times, the very role which we already know is
played by Claudio Goli (p.163):

> Y así empezó (he caído varias veces en esa tentación) una quincena
> de excesos, delirios, arrebato y pasión romántica, que pues conlleva
> teatro, jamás se sabe dónde comienza verdad y fingimiento. Por
> ventura siempre he sabido, de repente, que debía parar. Siempre se
> me desplomó el decorado antes que la obra. Pero los momentos de
> vigoroso placer, los momentos de vivir sólo por la vida son
> inigualables, vertiginosos, tan locamente únicos que los sabes excelsos,
> con la virtud y la desgracia de un veneno placentero. Fuimos a Niza
> unos diez días (yo había estado ya, varios veranos atrás, leyendo las
> memorias de Isadora Duncan y pagando a *ragazzi* del sur, que llevaban
> tangas ínfimos, enseñando el vello del púbis) e hicimos allí cuanto se
> le ocurrió a Gonzalo. Sólo la cama – hasta cierto punto – era mi reino.
> [...] Yo lucía a Gonzalo y él lo sabía. [...] Algo tenía de un Tadzio más
> germánico y mayor, pero no menos hermoso. Y su piel suave y blanca,
> su manera morbosa de hacer el amor, y sus miradas dulces y turbias,
> elegantes y rastreras al tiempo, todo lo aureolaba y abismaba en sus
> brazos. Pero comprendí (pese a la mucha pasión y exhibicionismo) que
> Gonzalo no tardaría mucho en dejarme pelado, y que – con la cuenta
> bancaria – se acabaría el mutuo gozo. Así es que, al volver a Madrid,
> y tras unos días en que seguimos igual, me distancié de Gonzalo.
> (p.169)

And thus (I have fallen into this temptation several times) started a
fortnight of excess, delirious surrender, romantic passion, which since
it always has something of the theatrical to it makes it impossible to
tell where truth and pretence begin or end. Luckily there has always
come a moment when I have suddenly known I ought to stop. With
me the set has always collapsed before the play was over. But those
moments of energetic pleasure, moments when you are living for life
itself, cannot be equalled, they are so dizzying, so crazily unique that
you know them to be supreme, laced with the virtue and mischance
of a gentle poison. We went to Nice for some ten days (I had been there
once before, some summers back, reading the memoirs of Isadora

Duncan and paying for the company of young southern *ragazzi* in tiny
tangas which showed their pubic hair) and there we did whatever
Gonzalo proposed. Only the bed – to a certain extent – was my realm.
[...] I was showing Gonzalo off, and he knew it. [...] There was
something of a Tadzio about him, more Germanic and more grown-
up but no less lovely. And his soft, white skin, his perverse and
knowing ways of making love, and the clouded and gentle looks he
gave, at once both elegant and debased, gilded all things and sent them
hurtling into the depths in his embrace. But I realised (despite all the
passion and the exhibitionism) that it would not be long before
Gonzalo would leave me penniless, and that our mutual enjoyment –
along with my bank account – would come to an end. So it was that
when we returned to Madrid, and after a few days of continuing in
the same way, I distanced myself from Gonzalo.

Once again we are led by a narrator whose hindsight allows
subtle comings and goings between the realms of sincerity and
flagrant inauthenticity. From one aesthetic position – dandified and
posed – the reference to Isadora Duncan, even in its equivocal
relation to the attractively vulgar detail of the *ragazzi*, adds glamour
to passion. From another – a position spiked with a sense of the
absurd – the episode is rounded by the banality of inevitability so
that the unique Gonzalo and the heady days of adventurous bliss
are just another romance, just another headspin towards an
overdraft. The aside on romantic passion ('which of course always
has something of the theatrical to it') points up the narrator's
awareness of his dual presence as the puppet of love and the scene-
setter and director. There is considerable switch of frame from a
blinkered and confident narrator (constructing the character
Gonzalo and arranging the sex scene) to a confessional and quite
unstarry-eyed wiser observer. His theatricality extends beyond his
narrated behaviour and into the narration itself, and the remark
about the collapse of the set is more than mere wry self-deprecation:
it points to a narrative strategy which sets up everyone for a fall,
including the narrator himself, and this gives a special piquancy.
The boys in their tanga thongs both blight and give a further lift to
the exalted Tadzio Gonzalo who has replaced them in the narrator's
affections; the banality of financial facts of life both mock and point
up the pleasures of the interlude they close as well as framing the
narrator as admirably unabashed sugar-daddy.

The self-destabilising act is, however, knowing and controlled.
Gonzalo will never escape fully his iconic status, he is too burdened

with images which refer elsewhere: to art, to gay experience (which after all he does not identify with), and to many other boys in Villena's writings who, being so like Gonzalo, steal his fire. The adoration of Gonzalo's body brings with it risky flirtations with politically unacceptable positions and inauthentic, if far from dull, representations of the narrating self. Bonding with the supposedly uncomplicated male body implies sending contemporary sexual politics into oblivion and valuing the hieratically heroic. It means loving 'the primitive', as in the cases of Santi, Sixto and Javier. And yet this flight from history, this denial of political responsibility and exaltation of the barbaric over the civilised, brings the civilised, the cultured, tracking back and cannot be enacted without it. Álvaro, in *Beyond the World*, depends on his bookish and aesthetic ideas for the full effects of his nostalgia for the abyss, the relationships with Santi and Gonzalo have to be written in theatrical and cinematic terms in order to return to the realm of the pre-civilised. The focus on the body leads, in effect, towards an exacerbated, excessive attention to the surface textures of culture, towards a calculatedly sentimental aesthetic in which emotional and intellectual abandon confuses the counter- or anti-cultural with the cultural, the pleasures of the body with the pleasures of the text. Such mixes and uncertainties become perversely liberating and perversely constricting as they challenge and engage with established cultural notions of authenticity, the relationship of art to life, wholeness and fulfilment, progress and transcendence. At his most serious Villena is prepared to abandon all such serious notions in their hallowed forms.

6

Abandon and Ecstasy

The Sentimental

The prevalence in Villena's poetry of ecstasy in the text and his willingness to address very closely a fascination with the most blatant stimuli of desire construct many moments of abandonment of literary, political, moral or emotional decorum, as we have already seen. The poems of escape are happy to alight, self-consciously and shamelessly, on both exoticism and obviousness. Idealisations are pre-subverted by an undertow of delightful, potent banality. Sensation – bodily and dramatic – is to the fore, and revelations (which may be breathtaking linguistic feats or emotional confessions) are the currency. Literary daring flirts closely not only with correctively self-aware parodic excesses but, inextricably perhaps, with the sentimental too. 'The prurient; the morbid; the wishful; the snobbish; the knowing; the arch: these denote sub-categories of the sentimental', suggests Sedgwick,[1] and as in Arturo's confession, so also in many of Villena's poems are these denotations activated. For Sedgwick the denotation occurs 'to the extent that each [of these sub-categories] involves a covert reason for, or extent or direction of, identification through a spectatorial route' (*Epistemology*, p.151). That is to say (less precisely), that scenes and stories like this (morbid ones, wishful ones and so on) let us gaze on them with grateful tears and know we are both ashamed and pleased to be identified and yet also (because mere spectators, readers or voyeurs) pleased to be apart from such goings on and such emotions. A vital element of the sentimental is a set of 'relations of vicariousness' (p.150) and this element is very strong indeed in some of Villena's texts, as the unveiled denotations of theatricality, unreliability, and impassioned partiality leave us clearly to understand.

1. Eve Sedgwick, *Epistemology of the Closet*, New York, 1990, p.151.

The ending of Arturo's account of his story in *Amour Passion* is a case in point. It is given a curious and complicated twist by the writing of a poem which addresses both implicitly and explicitly the destabilising potential of cliché, sentimentality and excess. The poem, with the naive shamelessness of a first poem, which is what Arturo says it is, is entitled 'Amor imposible' ('Impossible Love') and has echoes, 'albeit it poor ones only' thinks Arturo (*Amor pasión*, p.89), of 'a new book, *Hymnica*, which I liked very much, although I was surprised to learn that it was by the circumspect and frivolous young man with glasses whom Sixto had greeted on the night of the dinner jackets years ago' (p.89). Villena, already glimpsed at the gala disco (see Chapter Four), is to appear once more in the story, towards the end of the text of César's response, in the chapter headed 'César: La final serenidad' ('César: Ultimate Serenity'). The setting is an old-fashioned café where Arturo and César have met up with Sixto, now back from Ibiza where he has (banally) been working as a waiter. Sixto (who knows Villena) introduces them, and Arturo, getting on well with him (an interesting pointer to his true sexual and ethical orientations), tells him the outline of his story:

> El de las gafas le fue oyendo con una sonrisa seria. Y cuando Arturo concluyó, le dijo: *Querido, detalle quitado o puesto (y no diré los que no me pertenecen) me has contado mi propia historia. También yo hoy, de algún modo, quería despedirme y desear buena suerte a Sixto.*
>
> Los muchachos sonreían – con clara admiración – pero el hablante, al poner punto, dirigió su mirada a una broncínea escultura. ¿No es curioso? ¿No volvía a convertirse la vida – con mejor o peor certeza – en un íntimo teatro? (p.104)

> The man in glasses listened with a serious smile on his face. And when Arturo finished he said, 'Well, my dear, give or take one or two details (and I am not saying which correspond to my own experience) it is my own story that you have just told me. I too, in a way, wanted to say good-bye today to Sixto and to wish him luck.
>
> The boys who were with him smiled – in obvious admiration – but the speaker, having put a full-stop to what he had to say, directed his gaze towards a bronze sculpture in the corner. Is it not odd? Had life not transformed itself once again – more or less accurately – into an enclosed and private theatre?

This pirouette of self-reference by the supra-narrator Villena dignifies Arturo's position and undermines it all at once. His feelings are justified by their being shared (and shared by a poet too) but threatened by association with the theatricality, the affectation (that amusing studied look away to the statue in the corner, signifying the 'escape' into culture) and, of course, with this open area of the homosexual cultural spectrum where evasion shades into directness, obviousness into remarkable peculiarity, shared experience into individuality.

It is into just this equivocal space and this cultural complex that Arturo's writing of his excessive poem is going to plunge him. For its echoes are strong and premonitory: its sentimentality, if not its uneven progress, is something Villena himself turns to in his later poems. Ghosting Villena poorly, Arturo writes:

> Qué absurdo sentimiento. Reconstruyo paso a paso
> nuestra historia. Me reprocho no haberte dado más [...]
> Me reprocho (aunque
> me gustases tanto) no haberme espoleado a quererte,
> a arrastrarme ante ti o contigo ante quien fuese . . .
> Me reprocho mi idealismo siendo tú tan perfecta materia.
> Y ahora que te veo (dos años después de la vez última)
> a punto casi ya de no gustarme (a pesar de tus ojos y de tu cuerpo aún
>   vivo) ahora 'amor mío'
> (excúsame esta tópica frase, excúsame la atroz sensiblería)
> ahora quisiera salvarte para siempre.
>
> (pp.89–90)

How absurd, this feeling. Step by step I reconstruct / our story. I reproach myself for giving you no more / [...] / I reproach myself (although / you attracted me so much) for not having urged myself to love you, / to crawl before you or crawl with you before whoever it might be . . . / Being, as you were, such perfect substance I regret my idealism too. / And now that I see you (two years since that last time) / now almost on the verge of not attracting me (in spite of your eyes and your body, full of life still) now 'my love' / (excuse this clichéd phrase, excuse the appalling sentimental tone) / I wish I could save you for eternity.

Arturo's poem begins with a half-attempt at some of the rhetorical, metrical and rhythmic structures of Spanish Romantic poetry. The initial grand tone, and some grand abstractions (daring, violence, depth, immensity, salvation, splendour), are abandoned in the swift descent into an outpouring of feeling which is both referred to apologetically and, nonetheless, unmitigated.

One of Villena's most interesting and challenging obsessions in the poetry written after *Amour Passion* is with just such shifts in sentiment, sincerity and sentimentality, shifts which are prompted by excesses in feeling, reference and expression. These difficult constructions in the sphere of sentimentality can be seen at work in a highly excessive recent text of Villena's, one about Love personified, 'Caravanas de oriente' ('Caravans of the Orient'), in *As To a Foreign Place* (*Lugar extraño*, pp.49–50):

Creíá (o pensaba saber) que éramos
hedonistas, paganos, atrapadores perpetuos del fugitivo instante,
y juzgaba que nada era mejor que ese placer de fuego.
A mis amigos jóvenes les daba sus caprichos, llenábamos
la casa de zarabanda y júbilo, y los cuerpos, buscándose,
se deslizaban por alfombras y lechos, rumbo hacia la delicia . . .
Pude creer (muchas veces) que vivía a mi modo un paraíso.
Mas un día, mientras la fiesta transcurría hermosa,
(gentiles cuerpos nuevos y amigos tan dichosos como siempre)
creimos oir el bizarro tintineo de extraña comitiva.
Era una música lejana, perturbadora y leve.
Y atraídos por ella (con las copas aún llenas en la mano)
ascendimos todos a la terraza para ver lo que fuera . . .
Y lo vimos. Y creció la música y el batintín exótico,
y al pronto se fue nuestra alegría, quedamos como inertes,
contemplando, mientras la regia comitiva cruzaba nuestros ojos.
No se detuvo. Pienso que ni nos miraron. Iban, desde luego,
hacia un lugar remoto, y venían, nadie sabe de dónde:
Una lujosa caravana, alegre y auroral como un río en estío,
cuya vista hechiza sin permitir análisis banales . . .
Supimos que aquello era el Amor. Y nos vimos en la terraza,
vestidos de fiesta, solos tristes, inútiles objetos sin sentido.

Este alegórico esbozo de lo que pienso es ahora mi vida
lo conté una noche, charlando, a camaradas de otras correrías.
Pero ellos no supieron (pues pondrá cada cual su propia imagen)
que tú eras ese Amor, y generó tu presencia las distantes metáforas.
Tú (veintiún años) que te entregas al mundo para apurarlo
a fondo, que amas las palabras y detestas lo *snob*,
que jamás has estado en mi festiva casa

I believed (or thought I knew) we all were / pagans, hedonists, perpetual hunters of the fugitive moment, / and I deemed that nothing could better the pleasures of fire. / I indulged my young friends in their whims, we filled / the house with swirling dance and joy, and bodies, seeking one another out / rolled on carpets and on beds towards delicious pleasure . . . / I was able (often) to think I lived in my way in paradise. / But one day, while the party moved along its handsome course, / (new graceful bodies and friends as happy as they always were) / we thought we heard the gallant tinkling sound of some strange cortège. / It was a distant, slight, disturbing music. / And drawn to it (with glasses still full in our hands) / we went up to the terrace to look down and see . . . / And we saw. And the music grew in strength and the noise of a gong was exotic on the air, / and at once our happiness was gone, we stood as if inert / in contemplation, while this princely retinue went past our eyes. / It did not stop. I think they did not even look at us. They were on their way / to a distant place, of course, and had come from who knows where: / A sumptuous caravan, full of happiness and morning light as a river in summer, / the sight of which enchants precluding all banal analysis . . . / We knew this was Love. And we saw ourselves on the terrace there / dressed for a party, solitary, sad, futile, senseless objects. / One night in conversation with quite another group of friends / I sketched this allegory of what I think is now my life. / But they didn't know (since each will put a different image to the story) / that this figure of Love was you and that your presence spawned those distant metaphors. / You (at twenty-one) the boy who surrenders to the world to drink it deep, / who loves words and loathes snobs, / who was never in my festive house.

The caravans come out of the *fin-de-siècle* and are specifically reminiscent of the *modernista* poet Rubén Darío; the social life seems to come out the 1920s; but a further slant might come out of our reading of the episode also as a camp transgression. Dollimore is at one stage concerned 'with that mode of camp which undermines the categories which exclude it' and with Oscar Wilde's linkage of 'paradox in the sphere of thought' with 'perversity in the sphere of passion' (*Sexual Dissidence*, pp. 309 and 310); he sees this as a 'version' of the connection 'between sexual perversion and social subversion' and reminds us of the significance of 'the masquerade of camp' (pp.309 and 311). The speaker in this poem is the host of an orgiastic party and the spectator of a sumptuous parade in the street outside. Surrendering to the spectacle, he dons the mask of escape, invoking that 'river in summer, / the sight of which enchants precluding all banal analysis' and gesturing to the utopia of emptiness and ecstasy, that old familiar space of unknowing. There is much of the carnivalesque to the poem's scenes (especially in the Venetian sense) and in the image of the boy whose 'presence spawned those distant metaphors' there is a subversion through the suggested surrender of textual control. Dollimore's interpretation of camp as '[undermining] the depth-model of identity from inside, being a kind of parody and mimicry which hollows out from within, making depth recede into its surfaces' (p.310) might fit Villena well, with his challenging theatricalities and self-framings, his preparedness to swoon into complicity with the apparently banal, to glory in the sensual, in the highly intertextual, in the surface, the polished and unreal perfect body. Villena in love abandons depth in embracing it, and in texts like 'Caravans of the Orient' he is writing profoundly in the recesses of superficiality.

The poem ends with the shamelessly excessive question put to the listening twenty-one-year-old and, vicariously, to us, '¿Podría un mendigo unirse al cortejo de un rey si pasara a su lado?' (*Lugar extraño*, p.50: 'Could then a beggar join the cortège of a king if it passed by his side?'), and the question turns its assumptions inside out, reinscribing them; the regality of the style beggars all possibility of sustaining the myth of the poet as inferior. Looking down into the street with his friends was not just (if at all) a search for a deeper meaning or for Love, but a way of looking down on love the cultural convention, seeing it and the loving writing self as enrichingly absurd. The removal of this mask at the end of the performance is both a defiance and a defence.

This complicated set of gestures is also at work in 'El amor es siempre de veras' ('Love Is Always Real') (pp.35–7) where once again desire is being very emphatically framed. The poem tells a sentimental story which sets up some interesting angles or 'relations of vicariousness' for the onlooking reader. The speaker is ostensibly talking to a younger man, in tears beside him, rehearsing the boy's crisis, and as if writing him a part for the future; most of all he is peeping into his private life through his projections and inventions:

> ¿Y qué ocurre si el amor no llega?
> Pues, como el refrán dice, hay que pintarlo.
> *Sin amor no es posible vivir*: Historia vieja. [...]
> Sin amor, porque celeste o divino lo anhelas,
> sin amor porque concluyó
> o porque no encuentras tu media naranja comprensiva
> (tan difícil a poco que te llames exigente)
> de un modo u otro, a inventarlo te dispones.
> Tendrás celos de un amigo,
> creerás que la chica de la parada
> (y el autobús huyó tan velozmente)
> era – exactamente ella – la novia soñada

tantísimo tiempo . . .
Gemirás en la almohada, buscarás otra amiga y otra agenda,
requebrarás al muchacho de los ultramarinos,
perseguirás de oficio, y en los breves encuentros
del bar y de las noches – incluso en los más
rituales – tejerás otra *historia de amor*
de cinco horas – o acaso menos –
con noviazgo, intrigas, conquista, provocación,
más celos, e inevitable éxtasis erótico (pese a todo)
en un coche o en una colchoneta . . .
No, no somos una banda de histéricos.
(Algo desquiciados, solamente.)
Pero es que, vida mía, no se puede vivir sin amor.
Es más que aburrido, *horrible*, vivir sin amor.
Y entonces, noche a noche
(incordiando, urdiendo planes,
liando y sobornando taxistas, sonriendo al camarero,
invitando a copas, rogando y desdiciéndote)
te inventas el amor. Lo construyes, lo ensalzas.
Ah miseria dorada de un amor sin amor . . .
¡Cuánto sufrimiento en tres o cuatro noches,
cúanto éxtasis breve, cúanta, cúanta nostalgia!
Pero más de una ventaja ha de tener
(y el dinero no es noble desventaja):
Cada amanecer estás tú solo, libre y claro,
en el anchísimo reino de tus sábanas . . .
¡Compañero: Enjúguese un poquito tan ridículas lágrimas!

(pp.36–7)

And what if love does not appear? / Well, as the saying goes, just make it up. / *There is no living without love*: yes, it's an old story. [...] Loveless, because you yearn for love to be divine, celestial, / loveless just because it's ended / or because you cannot find your understanding other half / (so difficult if you're in the least demanding) / one way or another you set about inventing it: / You may be jealous of a friend, / think the girl at the bus-stop (and how rapidly that bus sped off) / was the one – the very one – the girlfriend you had so long dreamt of . . . / You will moan into your pillow, look for another girl, and start another diary, / and will flatter the boy in the grocery store, / make pursuit your speciality, and in brief encounters / in the bars, at night – in even the most ritual / of exchanges – you will weave another five-hour Love Affair / – or shorter even – with a courtship, / intrigue, conquest, provocation / jealousy again, and erotic ecstasy inevitably (all the same) / in a car or on a mattress . . . / No, we are not just a band of hysterical men. /

(Somewhat off-beam, nothing more.) / But you simply, my darling, cannot live without love. / It is, more than tedious, simply horrible to live without love. / So night by night / (making complicated plans and putting people out, / then screwing up, bribing taxi-drivers, smiling at the waiter, / buying drinks, begging then retracting) / you invent love for yourself. Construct and elevate it. / *Ah gilded wretchedness of a loveless love!* . . . / Such suffering in a night or two or three, / such brief ecstasy, and oh, such nostalgia! / But more than one advantage there must be in this / (and money is by no means a noble disadvantage): / Each dawn you are alone there, shining and free, / in the wide-flung realm of your bed . . . / Come on, my friend, dry those tears, those ridiculous tears!

The 'reality' of love, its high authenticity, is teased by the conscious banalities of the 'understanding other half', the girl at the bus-stop, the grocer's boy, the 'same old story' and by the little cliché (which I have stupidly disabled in translation) about 'if a thing does not exist, just make it up' (based on the Spanish 'si no hay, lo pintas' – literally 'if it isn't there, just paint it in'). The almost queeny-sharp remark about money makes a wry perspective (is he alone just because he will not spend the whole night with a punter?). The bisexuality of the boy addressed is also a tease: love might be 'always real', but its objects are always shifting, like that bus. As in all good sentimental seductions, sexiness and pity cut across each other: that moaning into the pillow and the closing focus on the solitary body in the bed at dawn really have us, like the speaker, wanting to reach out and dry those tears (or ours).

Love is reinscribed as the poem folds fondly into the mode of the diary entry, the speaker steadily approaches the boy, wants to draw him in to the circle of older gay men (the 'slightly off-beam') and himself move inside the boy's sex-life. The text turns out to be a less a sympathetic monologue more a meta-seduction, a newly-woven Love Affair in its own right, the very invention which is inscribed in love's 'reality'. Seeing sentimentality, as Eve Sedgwick suggests, 'not as a thematic or a particular subject matter, but as a structure of relation, typically one involving the author- or audience-relations of spectacle' (*Epistemology*, p.143) means seeing it here. It is a redemptive and a transgressive act to position the subject as wry, even cynical, confidant and as the vicarious adventurer and diarist; as the analyst looking over the shoulder of young love's foolish inauthenticity and as the ingenuous believer. The display of the boy's own story, the twice-displayed (if semi-wrapped) body and the play of tears activates a minor 'transgressive reinscription', a 'tracking back', as Dollimore puts it, 'of the 'other' into the 'same' [when] the proximate [has been] constructed as the other [...] in a process which facilitates displacement' (*Sexual Dissidence*, p.33). For here the Other, figured in the boy, is sentimentality, the (compelling) trashiness of the narratives of love, what decent folk and the high-minded want to keep away from them for very shame of their attractions. Figured in the watching and relating poet, the Other is also prurience, wishfulness, vicariousness, all part of what Sedgwick calls the 'quiverful of sub-categories' which sentimentality is likely to shoot out at the spectator of its scenes (*Epistemology*, p.152). Both the boy whose story is reported and the narrator are in the business of the reinvention, a remake, of love; the sentimental mode toys with the risk of exceeding love's authority, of losing control. In this reinvention, life becomes a spectacle and the whole fixed notion of genuine feelings (in other words acceptable feelings) is liberatingly questioned.

Death and Emptiness

The association between the excessive mode of expression and the paradoxical, perverse reinvention of the discourses of love constantly leads Villena's vital accounts of a new and different Spain back into considerations of death. In this he activates in the reader's mind, perhaps, received ideas about Spanishness and the Romantic spirit (a dark and popular linkage of love, blood and sand). He necessarily avoids falling into the clichéd role of a latter day Lorca, however, despite the deliberate connections between eroticism and death, beauty and decline and despite the wilful, apparent marginality of much of the writing. The essay 'On Suicide and Death', discussed in the Introduction, uses marginalisation to reverse a moralising, controlling discourse by calling Villena 'immature' and placing him alongside those who are 'not adapted to life' who flee the mediocre happiness of 'mature and normal people' (*Ícaro*, pp.94 and 95). This reversal is explicitly linked (p.97) to *Death Alone*, the volume read by José Olivio Jiménez as marking the establishment of a new seriousness ('La poesía', p.62). Here, the preference for dying carries over, metaphorically, into the realm of poetic practice and finds a new dissidence which flies in the face of straighter discourses while also embracing them. Just as the Villena analysed by Leopoldo Alas half wants his desire to be disembodied in a double spiral of 'quest and evasion' (Alas, 'Notas', p.147), so he half wants the search for the black moment of death to be not a sexual or a textual ecstasy only but at one with a grave, transcendental reculturing of love coming out of Renaissance humanism and blending with twentieth-century liberal humanist cultures which take love seriously and death profoundly. Such a seriousness and depth-orientation are symptomatic – as Dollimore argues in *Sexual Dissidence* – of a longing for stability, eternal truth, confirmation of essence and, above all, control. The epilogue to *Death Alone* reveals the temptation of such a discourse, but the risk which is taken here is anchored and countered by the body in the text: the goal of living through and for art is to

> Indagar en las apetencias y pasiones de la intrarrealidad, manteniendo el goce de los sentidos y la palpitación – algo falaz – de la apariencia material: palpar la música, beber sensaciones . . . Mas, por supuesto, caminar hacia el interior, anhelar que se trasponga el horizonte, levantar el velo. Platón o Fray Luis – evidentemente – no se engañaron. Y apetecer vivir (mientras se odia vivir) porque sólo de ti – y de ese tú asumido en cuerpo deseante – nace la Buena Muerte, la Muerte Apetecida y añorada. (*Poesía*, pp.343–4)

> Investigate the passions and the appetites of that underlying reality, the reality beyond, while maintaining the full enjoyment of the senses and the (somewhat false) pulsation of the appearance of material reality: to feel music, drink in sensations . . . But of course, move inwards too, long for a shift in the horizon, lift the veil. Plato or Fray Luis [de León] – evidently – were not mistaken. And to have an appetite for life (while hating to live) because only in you – and in you as a body desiring – may Good Death, Sweet and longed for Death be born.

This kind of dying to the self, this consciousness of 'you as a body desiring' is the prime dynamic in maintaining with the appropriate intensity the traffic between aesthetics and experience. As we have been seeing from *Death Alone* and *Beyond The World*, the flirtations with straight humanism Villena lets his voices indulge in are troubled and countered by this intensity and by the constant movement and interchange of soul and body, surface and depth, sentimental and sublime. In the end Villena's continuing investment in the 'text [as] pleasure embodied' (*Poesía*, p.115) is less a single, closed-off aesthetic position, more a multiple question; less an affiliation with the tradition of Romantic Spain or Decadent Europe, more a set of divergent possibilities. In *The Journey to Byzantium* these possibilities are explored through the posing of this multiple question in the poem 'Monumento en honor de Lord Byron' ('Monument in Honour of Lord Byron') (p.140): '¿Qué extraño lazo anuda sentimiento y deseo, / pensamiento y figura, concavidad y ritmo?' ('What strange bond links feeling and desire, / thought and figuration, concavity and rhythm?'). This hollow in the imagination – the classic modernist gap between feeling and expression – is, in the terms of this poem and of so many of the subsequent works, represented by the hand passing down and over the curves of the body. The rhythm is achieved in '[un] inmenso zumbido de las manos y los labios' ('[a] vast humming of hands and lips') which make sex and the utterance of poetry indistinguishable in these shifting horizons where text and desire, sex-experience and literary aesthetics writhe in a long Romantic embrace. As 'Beau Satan' (*Hymnica*) has it, 'La más dulce saliva prende un lazo de muerte, / el terso cuerpo tibio, la seducción suicida . . .' (p.194: 'The sweetest saliva draws out a ribbon of death, / the warm, tensed body, suicidal seduction . . .').

The hollow in the imagination is also – and how, given its provenance, could it be otherwise? – the abyss, the engulfing despair of the late Romantics, death. Again traditionally, the tensions between feeling and desire, desire and reality, are prone to lead to exhaustion, listlessness, *ennui* or emptiness, and much of Villena's writing acts in defiance of this. The difficulty of maintaining the necessary flame of intensity of textual yearning and thus postponing the fall into dullness, despair or conformity is illustrated disturbingly in *As To A Foreign Place*. Many of the poems here place more emphasis on unmitigated failure and acceptance of failing vitality than previous collections. The temptation to retreat from intensity, a siren call listened to in some of the texts of escape in earlier collections, is now much stronger. The first poem, 'Encomio a un amigo, en su total renucia' ('Encomium for A Friend, In His Complete Renunciation') (*Lugar extraño*, pp.9–11) notes, in praising this unnamed friend in monastic retreat, how 'El Arte es lo más arduo, y va contra la vida' (p.10: 'Art is the hardest task and goes against life'). It is not now a question of glorifying the Byronic quest, for the friend is envied for being beyond the intensity of the attempt, and being, like a sage from an earlier era, 'Ajeno a la vida y la acción' (p.11: 'Removed from life and action.'). 'Et omnia vanitas' (p.21), whose title goes even further back than the echoes of the sixteenth century in the 'Encomio . . .', narrates the retirement of a dandy, one who – like Huysmans's Des Esseintes – is now, in his retreat, scarcely recognisable: '¿Es este [...] / El escandaloso, buscador de extravagancia?' ('can this be [...] / he who once lived a scandalous life in search of extravagance?' The poem 'En el invierno romano' ('In the Roman Winter') (pp.17–18) appears to rewrite the sentiments of the earlier more vital collection of stories of the same name by centring on the image of a jaded aesthete who delights in remaining in bed with books and brandy and memories while outside, in a chronological swirl, all the tales of the fall of empires are acted out: eunuchs, mosaics, Rhenish hordes, tax problems, frosts on the fruit harvest, the fishing fleet on strike, friends who have retreated to their farms, knifings in the metro and puddles of beer spilled out on dance-floors, all pass by as the speaker sips his brandy and reads another line of lyric verse.

Similarly theatrical and similarly unstable is 'Álvaro de Campos se mira' ('Álvaro de Campos Considers Himself') (pp.69–70),[2] a self-conscious monologue in which all the values of dissidence are affirmed, but from the point of view of disenchantment and studied indifference. Here the argument for the culture of dandyism loops back on itself: Álvaro de Campos in his wryness (and Villena in his), bidding himself a stylised farewell as he puts on his gloves in front of the mirror, casts some doubt on the old creed restated here 'Hay que darse a todos los placeres / [...] / escandalizar con erotismo' (p.7: 'you must give yourself over to every pleasure / [...] / 'scandalise with eroticism'). The poem ends with a tonally evasive 'Gracias, señor De Campos. Siga bien. / Ah, y no me sonría . . .' (p.7: Thank you, señor De Campos. Keep well, sir. / Ah, and do not smile at me . . .').This is the perfect, the textbook dandified stance. To be impassive is central to 'the ethics of dandyism [...] by which the dandy exercises his difference in all its (aesthetic) rigour' according to the analysis of Cernuda in *Corsairs in Yellow Gloves* (*Corsarios*, p.131), but this means that through 'a very dandyistic paradox [...] at the same time as cultivating and heightening his sense of self [the dandy] wishes to hide and has to hide his most intimate cares'

2. Álvaro de Campos is one of the pseudonyms of the Portuguese poet Fernando de Pessoa.

(p.132). The dandy's rebellion (and especially Cernuda's in the context of this essay) is predicated on and constructs desire but also depends on a sublimation of feelings, a disembodying of desire. Cernuda and the dandy as constructed by Villena have already gone in a sense too far, beyond the senses, the body, the common and the sentimental. Calm, icy or embittered recollection – the distanced focus which both realises and idealises the conventional notion of desire – will not sustain the dynamic which allows ecstasy to be embodied. To be ready to embrace the notion of death and eschew the imperfections of life to this degree is to abandon both the body and the text.

In the second section of 'Patria mía' ('Country of Mine') from *Death Alone* (*Poesía*, pp.315–17) (the first section of which refers to Spain with an oblique allusion to Cernuda's 'Elegía española I', 'Spanish Elegy, I'),[3] death is at first figured allegorically as the site of ultimate rest and distance from the sensual world. But the poem soon shifts towards a very different territory, one which is warm, sentimental, lively, sexy and very self-consciously of this world:

> Como quien mete las manos en una fuente tibia,
> conviene cada día humedecerse de tu sombra,
> acariciar el agua oscura que hay detrás de todo,
> y besar esa bruma como si labios fuese.
> [...]
> Mas si tuviese el Universo un átomo tan sólo de equidad
> o bondad mínima, allí me aguardarían tus ojos y tu voz,
> y acurrucado en ti, contigo y con tu cuerpo
> me iría entre tus brazos, inmarchitable amor,
> abajo, muy abajo, por el eterno río
> de esta patria profunda:
> Solos los dos, entre muchos, navegando.
>
> (pp.316–17)

Like one who dips his hands in a spring of warm water, / one should every day be moistened by your shadow, / caress the dark and underlying water, / and kiss the curling mist as though it were lips. / [...] / But if the Universe had just an atom of justice / or the smallest mercy, there would your eyes and your voice be waiting for me, / and hugging close to you, with you, with your body / I would fall away in your arms, my imperishable love / down, deep down along the eternal river / of this our profoundest home: / The two of us alone, with many others, sailing off.

3. Cernuda, *Poesía*, p.212.

The abstract body of death then shades into the familiar – and potently invoked – body of the lover of our dreams. The flagrantly wishful image of the lovers on the river echoes all those other scenes of boys on eroticised pastoral adventures in the country, out at sea. In an earlier, and more plainly sexy, poem 'Mística de dioses antiguos' ('The Mysticism of Ancient Gods') in *To Flee from Winter* (pp.217–18) sex, love, death, and evasion (explicitly to the coded south) are cast into a wishful, prospective and seductive conditional, the same device used in 'Country of Mine':

> Yo moriría, creedme, me iría muriendo,
> si alcanzase ese sur, tus ojos grandes,
> y el ámbito sin cambio de esa hermosa amistad,
> cómplice como un beber de dos marineros.

(pp.217–18)

> I should die, believe me, I should slowly die, / if I were to reach that southern place, your large wide eyes, / the unchanging space of that lovely friendship, / as complicit as two sailors together drinking.

The poem then crosses over from these gay young tars into a concluding section (p.218) on an incident in Eunapius's *Lives of the Philosophers* where Porphyry, moved by Plotinus's disquisition on the soul, desires to die, to free his own soul from his body. This strange juxtaposition is a characteristic cultural transgression, marking death as a site of transition not from life into nothingness but – in perpetual interchange – of seriousness into excess, idealism into sentimentality, intellectualisation into sexiness.

The treatment of Leopoldo, in *Boys*, is a stimulating instance of this double movement. When his story begins he is given status as the image of life in death and the epitome of true – that is to say unrealised – desire and is framed not only as implicitly (another) perfect form but also disruptively as soft-porn picture:

> Creo que fue el verano pasado. Chanceando cierto amigo y yo, propusimos adelantar cuál sería la última imagen (no la última frase) de nuestras postremías. ¿En qué pensará uno, en el momento final, al borde de la muerte y su negrura? Y dije que en tal *desideratum* lo más normal me parecía pensar en algo que hubiéramos deseado mucho, incluso tenido casi al alcance de la mano, pero que no se hubiera cumplido, dejándonos con la ansiedad de una fruta ofrecida. Esa anhelada insatisfacción, en mi lógica, debiera ser nuestra última (porque también conlleva frustración) y mejor imagen de la vida. Y como se me pidió concretar, conté, que muriéndome, vendría a mi

mente la bella imagen de Leopoldo, sorprendidos los ojos, el pelo cayéndole en la frente, y a punto de quitarse los calcetines. (*Chicos*, p.73)

It was, I think, last summer. Joking together, a friend and I proposed that each should look ahead to what would be the last image (not the last words) accompanying our final moments. What would one think of, in the final moment, on the edge of death and darkness? And I said that in such an eventuality it seemed to me that it would be most normal to think of something we had desired a lot, even had within reach, but which had never been obtained, leaving us with the yearning for fruit proffered but withheld. Such longed for lack of fulfilment as this should, according to my way of thinking, be our last (because it also implied frustration) and our best image of life. And since I was being asked to be precise, I told him that when I was dying the lovely image of Leopoldo would come to me, with surprise in his eyes, his hair falling down over his forehead, and bending to take off his socks.

The surprise in Leopoldo's eyes is due to the narrator's eventual refusal, after many timid hours of obvious desire, to be seduced into bed and sex. He – like Villena according to Alas ('Notas') – knows that the desire of that moment, like all desire, is touched by impossibility; that if it were not, then it would not be desire. He knows – and constructs the idea – that Leopoldo is more important as an emblem of the falling away of things, of love-in-death; he is also our guide in an allegory, showing us the story of the end of an era (his story is full of references to the good days of the 1970s now gone) but pointing the way towards a utopian sexuality and ethics. The postponement of the fall into cultural conventionality is sustained by the narrator's refusal to engage with the glossy, soft-porn image of Leopoldo. To surrender to the desires constructed by such an easy image would be to betray the spirit of rebellion. The image of Leopoldo keeps at a distance both dandified indifference and programmed sexual impulse, both the banality of unmediated experience, mere life, and the hollowness of a death which is no more than a fading away. Ready to remove his clothes, he stands at the impossible intersection of postponement and fulfilment, revealing the cultural as well as the emotional restlessness and undecidability of Villena's writing.

The Emptiness of Grandeur

The 'last image' of Leopoldo is also one which invites questions about his status as an enduring symbol of perfect living beauty. His story is one which tarnishes him in its telling. It satirises the world from which Leopoldo and, indeed, the narrator get their reflected glory, wrily taking to task both grand-queenery and youthful arrogance. Through this narrative framing it invites Villena and his readers again to assess where – if anywhere – the dividing lines might lie between exclusiveness and pretentiousness, stylishness and vulgarity, attractiveness and intolerability, vitality and dull death. It is a story constructed around considerable uncertainties.

The narrator first notices Leopoldo in the discothèque Bocaccio and begins to be fascinated by him. He is, in the early pages of the story, established as 'mysterious, ambiguous', 'indecipherable', 'special', 'remote, distant, and, perhaps for that very reason, attractive to a high degree' (pp.73–5). He is eighteen, his hair is dark and long, and his sexuality delicately ambiguous. Even his class is indefinable and the narrator senses 'a contradiction, perhaps a forceful one, but one only perceptible to the most highly trained sensitivities,' a hint of working-class origins beneath his present distinguished air: 'it was never quite clear – whether student, queen, rent boy, actor, thief or count – where to place him' (pp.74 and 75). He is seen in the company of the Marquis of Mircigada ('a notorious lover of boys': p.75) and Carlos Capote, a dealer in fine art and antiques, but his sexual status remains undefined: 'he didn't seem to be a person who would fit into fixed types. Perhaps he was not even an adept of the world of homophilia. Although that was more doubtful, being where he was when he was' (p.76). With a sharp sense of class distinction and in shameless reinforcement of his own homosexual exclusiveness (sex with women denoting a lack of sophistication again), the narrator reports that Capote and Mircigada know 'that some days he could not meet them because he was going out with his girlfriend. If he had himself used that word, "girlfriend" (*"novia"*), then I would be right to imagine there were working-class roots there alongside the supposed *haute bourgeoise* air of distinction' (p.76).

The narrator's fascination increases one late night at an orgiastic party in Capote's house where Leopoldo is set upon and his shirt removed ('a strong, fine chest, very white despite the summer and skin which seemed so smooth that it became the very stuff of lust and of the desire to touch' (p.79); he enjoys this, but resists further attentions, 'So the mystery surrounding Leopoldo had to do with these two facts of life: desire and control; provocation and evasion' (p.80). In Leopoldo's chest, then, beats the heart of Villena's exploitations of the perverse dynamics of 'life'.

Leopoldo is taken up by Elmyr d'Hory (a counterfeiter of fine art and the subject of Orson Welles's last film *Fake*) and then by Miguel Gresola, a wealthy and prominent aristocrat from Valencia, who takes him to Paris. Here the story is taken over by Mircigada, giving the telling of the tale an interesting twist, for now much of it is channelled through a personality whose probity is in doubt and whom, at the narrator's prompting, we cannot take seriously. One of a long line of distressed gentlemen in Spanish literature since *Lazarillo de Tormes*, Mircigada is a gentleman down on his luck, and down in everyone's esteem too:

> un personajillo conocido por entonces en los entresijos de la noche madrileña: Joven que no lo aparentaba, de fea nariz aguileña, bigotillo cuarentón y andares de señorito andaluz, el Marqués de Mircigada era un notorio pederasta, que nunca apeaba su apostura, aunque se rumoreaba (utilizando su mote femenino, sacado del apellido) que no tenía un duro. Lo que debía ser verdad, pues – años después – tuvo que ponerse a trabajar en lo que fuera. (p.75)

> a minor personality known round and about in those days in the nooks and crannies of Madrid night-life, young without looking it, with an ugly hooked nose, a forty-year-old's moustache and the gait of the Andalusian idle rich, the Marquis of Mircigada was a notorious lover of boys who always maintained an air of elegance although people said (changing his title into a fem nickname) that he hadn't got a penny. Which must have been true, since years later he eventually had to take work wherever he could get it.

On the occasion of the orgy Mircigada fares no better at the narrator's hands: 'They were all looking [at Leopoldo] like so many greedy lizards [...] and Mircigada, round-bellied and sweating, more than anyone else' (p.79). Starkly contrasted with the pure beauty of the unshirted Leopoldo, Mircigada is seen before him 'kneeling, panting' (p.79) and very much an obstacle to the narrator's proper enjoyment of the moment. Mircigada, then, is in this sense an unreliable narrator: not only unstable and likely to embellish but unflatteringly lit and unfairly represented by the text.

Central to the Paris episode as recounted by Mircigada is an evening when out to dinner at Maxim's restaurant with Gresola, Leopoldo attracts the attention of fellow-diner Franco Zeffirelli. A fierce quarrel ensues, with Gresola, in front of all the other diners, calling Zeffirelli, a 'queer' ('maricón') and declaring 'If you don't leave the boy alone, you dirty slut, I'll kill you' ('*Si no dejas en paz al chico, zorra de mierda, te mato*': p.86). All this 'at the top of his voice, in Spanish' (p.86) which adds to the humour, since neither Zeffirelli nor most of the other diners could understand anything of this, though Zeffirelli 'knew, obviously, what it was about' (p.86). A reference in the text to Mircigada's own skill at mimicking Gresola (p.86) allows us easily to guess at the relish with which the tale is being told, to picture the graceless teller, and to see plainly that this is the grand queen's tale *par excellence*. The film-maker's defiant words, as he sweeps out, leaving Leopoldo his card and just avoiding the shower of wine Gresola has flung at him, are, in the context, arch and entertaining: '*Chiamami, caro. Bello, certo, molto bello.*' These italicised words – imputed, as it were, at two removes – share narrative space with a whole jewellery-box-load of other foreign and exotic words which set the tone: '[el] *tout Paris*', '*boîte*' '*maître*', Zeffirelli referred to obliquely as 'the refined *regista* of *Romeo and Juliet*,' the snobby anglicism '*smoking*' (for dinner-jacket), a reception '*chez* Polignac', and, of course, three times, *Maxim's*, italicised and with its own snobby little anglicism into the bargain (pp.84–6). All of this, though, raises questions about how distant the principal narrator and Mircigada really are, and it prompts the suspicion that the former is in love with what he is asking us to laugh at (just, indeed, as he is as much bewitched by Leopoldo as is the absurd and grotesque Mircigada). The narratorial relationship to the exotic and the exclusive is problematic, here as elsewhere in Villena's writing. There seems no doubt that if Mircigada recounts the Paris incident 'doubled up with laughter, and probably envy too' (p.86) Villena might well have wished he also had been there.

In fact he does send his narrator to Paris. This journey is one that is encoded by a Spanish tradition a century-and-a-half long of trips in search of Culture, romance, excitement and an escape from the drabness of Madrid; and the visit is an opening socially, sexually and thematically for the narrator. It also matches Villena's own story as narrated in *In Front of the Mirror* (*Ante el espejo*, pp.137–53), further complicating the scene of desire. In Paris the narrator is able to hear the Gresola-Zeffirelli story again, from acquaintances of his art-world friends there. One of those retelling the story is a 'prominent French monarchist leader with an *ancien régime* title' (*Chicos*, p.89) and he it is who brings to the tale a detail which for the narrator redeems Gresola: 'when the monarchist asked our duke how he had allowed himself to get so very carried away by his impulses [...] Gresola replied, very gravely (and the Frenchman laughed as he related this): *But my dear, I did it out of passion*' (p.89). The aristocratic presence, the excessive emotion, and the mantle of the Maxim's-and-grand queens' atmosphere fall like a blessing on Gresola and the narrator alike: 'It was – despite it all – a noble gesture. A move which made Gresola more agreeable to me when previously he had seemed just a boorish nuisance with Francoist undertones' (p.89). Even more importantly, this trip to Paris and this contact at last gives the narrator access to Leopoldo's full esteem. The next time they meet (in Time) Paris is the key, and they start swapping reminiscences and names:

> dimos marcha a la conversación inerte, la aupamos, y sin proponérnoslo, llegamos a París. Me contó que había estado allí no hacía mucho, y le respondí lo mismo. Y entonces realizamos un tópico viaje turístico proclamando las delicias de la *Ville Lumière* [...] me dijo que conocía allí a mucha gente. Lo pronunció con cierto aire engolado e inocente, como insinuando, desde el inicio, que esa *gente* era la genuina, la única a la que merecía la pena conocer, la que – no sé si Morand o Proust – llamaron la *tribu suprema* [...] fue dejando caer algunos nombres de amigos a los que atribuía – inocentemente – plena familiaridad. (pp.90–1)

> we set the inanimate conversation in motion, hauled it up onto its feet, and, without planning to, we alighted on Paris. He told me he had been there not long before, and I said the same. We then started off on a clichéd tourist trip singing the delights of *la Ville Lumière* [...] he told me he knew a lot of people there. He emphasised this with a certain haughtiness and innocence as if wanting to hint from the start that these really were the genuine thing, the only *set* it was worth knowing, what Morand or Proust – I don't know which – called *the supreme tribe* [...] he kept dropping names claiming – ingenuously – complete familiarity with them.

When the narrator intimates that he too is familiar with some of these, Leopoldo is suddenly all seductive smiles, and 'it was as if, suddenly, he had taken from his pocket a folded piece of tissue, and had slowly been opening it out to let it float in the end like a veil to wrap me to his tender and captivating self' (p.91).

Leopoldo is undermined by the narrator's (also self-deflating) references to cliché and snobbery. His interpretation of Parisian life is destabilised by its juxtaposition to the Zeffirelli-Gresola incident where the exclusivity of dinner at Maxim's is developed into the farce which makes the episode just an everyday tale of artistic folk. Leopoldo's sense of the special begins to look increasingly naive. Despite the seductiveness of the image of Leopoldo in the passage just quoted, the narrator is not entirely taken in and we as readers are not required to take our exclusivism neat here any more than we are elsewhere. Leopoldo may look as if he has all the advantages, but textually he is outwitted. His uniqueness and enclosedness are threatened not only by the wry perspective on the Parisian queenery but also by his being little less than choreographed (a mini-Diaghilev), put on view, iconised as captivation itself. Although the Paris conversation-piece is the decisive step in the courtship, it is associated with the idea of a gilded world artfully tarnished by the slightly acid gaze of the narrator, the sense of perfection flawed by circumstance and Leopoldo's lack of real knowledge of the privileged life.

In another less equivocal direction, though, the Parisian association does have unspoilt utopian and counter-cultural resonances. A two-page essay on the leisured elite of the first half of the century is embedded in the story of Leopoldo between Mircigada's recounting of the Zeffirelli story and the narrator's own further discoveries about the incident during his own visit to Paris (pp.87–8). It describes lovingly the bohemians, artists and cultured aristocrats of the period prior to the Second World War living a fantastical, luxurious and orgiastic life in 'primitive little paradises on the shores of the Mediterranean' (p.87). Dalí is quoted on the subject (p.88) and in the post-war period the names are Orson Welles, Elmir d'Hory, Visconti, Zeffirelli, Cocteau, Tennessee Williams, Gresola along with the Guggenheims on the moneyed side and 'if we go a long way down the list [...] people like Mircigada or Capote' (p.87). Leopoldo, we are told, 'had an intuitive sense of this world and wanted to take part in what was left of it' (p.88), and this, to an extent, redeems him, making him not so much the hanger-on but more the poetic rebel, 'anxious to turn life into theatre, into art, into something immensely superior to flat and simple reality' (p.88).

This whole sequence – Mircigada's version; the essay on those happy few; the two sojourns in Paris – completes the network which supports the narrator's dreams and the story of Leopoldo. As Madrid is linked to Paris and the Mediterranean (European and African), the 1980s to the 1920s, this *fin-de-siècle* to the last, so Leopoldo becomes an icon alongside Rafael and Gonzalo. Not just a physically powerful image, he also lights the way between contemporary Madrid and that bygone era, between sex within a contemporary (if unacknowledged) popular gay culture and the grand narratives of a perversely counter-cultural elitism. Like Gonzalo he is made to signify a sense of an ending and, more than simply objectified and fixed, is inescapably inscribed and activated in a narrative of ecstasy and decline. Paradoxically and perversely the emptiness of grandeur proves to be the fulfilment of the reader's pleasure and the delight of author and narrator.

Decline and Perversity

In 'Gonzalo' another 'last image' – that of the fallen angel – marks an important transition, this time from desire to shame. The idolised Gonzalo-Heliogabalus in the second part of his story slips from his tower into this abyss, transformed from 'splendid, avenging angel' (p.174) into fallen angel. The descent is seductively and camply coded. Gonzalo is taken up by the very wealthy Antonio Carles who in his honour opens up his extravagantly sumptuous, eighteenth-century Madrid home to throw parties for 'the most beautiful and prestigious people of the underground scene and the *movida*' (p.175), one in which 'liveried servants offered cocaine around on trays' (p.175), or another 'where, in the indoor swimming pool (in a huge Egyptian-style salon covered in porphyry), the water was flavoured with strawberry cordial and various male models – truly sublime boys – bathed naked, covered in sweet water, inviting the guests, like nymphs, to join them' (p.176). 'Orgies of champagne, sex and drugs' (p.176) in silk-hung rooms soon tail off as Carles and Gonzalo take to heroin and to living in 'the light opera extravaganza of a house, almost a Medici fantasy, which his grandfather had had built at Salou' (p.178). This narrative turn reveals an interesting dynamic: the theatricality, which in other instances in *Boys* lightly exalts either the narrator or the scene it envelops, tilts towards absurdity and dismay. The language of the statuesque now marks a closure not an extension of vitality: visiting the two of them there by the sea, the narrator finds that hedonism has congealed, extremism has lost its fire, and Gonzalo has become quite numb. In a chilling scene on the siesta-hour terrace where Gonzalo lies dazed, the narrator, with a surge of sexual nostalgia, reaches out to touch him:

> comentando algo sobre el brillante color del mar, puse mi mano sobre el pecho dorado, marcado e impoluto del muchacho. Le acaricié y él ni me miró de nuevo. Tampoco hizo seña de desagrado. Entonces [...] me vi llevando esa mano a su entrepierna y, absurdamente, bajándole el pequeño pantalón y tomándole el sexo dormido. Gonzalo siguió inmutable. Tenía su rostro una dureza que me recordaba la del muchacho que conociera en *Love* pero transmutada en estatua. Me fui lleno de vergüenza, silencioso. (p.179)

> making some comment on the brilliant colour of the sea, I placed my hand on the boy's golden, shaped and unblemished chest. I caressed him and he didn't even look at me again. Nor did he show any sign of displeasure. Then [...] I found myself moving that hand down to between his legs and, absurdly, lowering his little shorts and taking hold of his dormant sex. Gonzalo remained impassive. His face had a hardness which reminded me of the boy I had once met in Love but transformed now into a statue. I left, filled with shame, and silent.

So much idealisation just petrifies into shame and silence, as if this particular trajectory of rebellion reverted to oppression, to the blankness of a static identity as outcast (both for narrator and narrated). Language is defeated, aesthetic sensibility is downgraded to being the mere verbal prelude to sexual advances, the iconography of the statuesque and perfect becomes blank matter; sex leads to a kind of death.

Conclusion

he pattern of attainment of genuine joy and the predictable and imminent fall from it – the double flight of Icarus – is the controlling pattern of Villena's writing as it soars and plummets between different cultures, attitudes and discourses. Rejecting conventional behaviour in writing and in sex, he also reaffirms a morbid and ironic love of it, and counter-culture fondly folds back in to culture. Death and the 'last images' with their ecstasies are part of a conventional cultural quest for the impossible realm but also – more interestingly – an undermining of the culture of high aestheticism, of humanist individualism, of metaphorical sexlessness. Villena's responses to 'true unattainable happiness' (*Ícaro*, pp.97–8) through sex and text involve both a recognition and a defiance of the power of such illusions.

Villena's is classic writing against the grain, its acts of rebellion are internalized, integral acts of faith: his very excessiveness is (in the homosexual cultural tradition) part of a consistent code, part of a reaction to 'life' which instils a proper sense of the importance of feints and fictions, fantasies and desires. As such it might be thought to be the ideal material of poetic writing as traditionally perceived; but lyricism is stretched to an ecstatic breaking point, idealism is teased as well as embraced, and form, decorum and seriousness are not delivered when apparently promised. This ruffles feathers. Villena has been accused of displaying 'too much erotic obsession' and 'amorous voyeurism' (in *Hymnica*).[1] He has conversely but just as inappropriately been claimed as an exemplar of sincerity, for the liberal humanist tradition and seen as creating 'a personal ethical code' out of 'erotic revelations' which have a redeeming cathartic effect,[2] and even José Olivio Jiménez's excellent essay on the poetry, when discussing the equivocal and

1. Florencio Martínez Ruiz, '*Hymnica*', *ABC*, 16 August 1979, p.22.
2. Fidel Vilar Robot, 'La consumación de la belleza', *El País*, 6 January 1980, 'Suplemento Letras', p.5.

many-sided *Death Alone*, risks overlooking the trangressive in a quest for (an undeniably important) moral seriousness: 'facing up to the most important question in life, [Villena now] chooses a different "cast" [...] from amongst those who have most deeply and seriously considered the existential problem of humanity [...]: Ficino, Quevedo, Marlowe, the Count of Villamediana' ('La poesía', p.62). Indeed, Villena's own taste for the more extravagant gestures and the most resonant names of literature can bring several mystifications down upon his head. His highly visible, self-advertising affiliations risk hasty compartmentalisation. It is all too easy to watch the texts drawing on the late Romantic, on the homoerotic tradition, Hellenism, the canonical texts of Spanish and European high culture, and become fascinated with the dynamic of reference, forgetting the originating gesture of the text which very often is carnivalesque, self-subverting, excessive, and, even, seriously camp. In particular his interest in Decadent writers and the marginalised or excluded is a temptation to the uneasy reader wanting too eagerly to find points of reference. Here, we can say, is a recognisable eccentric, or dandy, an Oscar Wilde, even the Lorca we never got to know because of his early death. Or, lamenting (because of the decadent affiliations) a proper gay political and correctly transgressive drive in these texts (and they are certainly no models of political any more than they are of sexual 'correctness'), we might search mystified for the sorts of positive images we expect of the sexually dissident text. But Andy Methurst reminds us in relation to readings of the carnivalesque that 'the very phrase ["positive images"] suggests a world of liberal fairness and bourgeois respectability that has never been on the agenda of carnival'[3] and we might turn his warning to considerations of Villena's masquerades too, adding that they know of this temptation and play with it. The ecstasy in the text, the scandal, coexist with and conform the seriousness and the revelations of loss. The harshness of dissident experience cannot be held off, but – because of this – the ecstatic, the sensual and the scandalous can persist.

The end of Álvaro's story, in *Beyond the World*, is exemplary of this. It echoes and intensifies the fate of so many of the other young heroes of Villena's narratives. Back in Madrid after the second journey, he becomes involved with a melancholy addict called

---

3. 'Carry On Camp', *Sight and Sound*, vol. 2, no. 4 (August 1992), pp.16–19, p.18.

Delfín, lives a brief, painful, drugged existence and dies in a knife-fight having got involved in drug-dealing. His wish is for his ashes to be scattered in the crater of Etna and Carlos and María comply. The novel ends equivocally, with an instability that perhaps reflects Villena's own dynamic indecision in this issue of the death-wish:

> fueron dejando caer, mansamente, con cierta voluptuosidad, las cenizas que fueron Álvaro, su amigo. No pensaron ni en poema ni en música (aunque hubiese sido una toma especialmente apta para un realizador melancólico), pensaron en la inutilidad y el vacío, pero también en la extraña plenitud que los recubre. Pensaron: ¿Adónde va la nave? ¿Qué raro pájaro canta en nuestro interior? ¿Hacia que senda volamos desordenadamente en un universo oscuro? (p.183)

> slowly, gently, and with a certain sensuousness, they let fall the ashes of what once was Álvaro their friend. They did not think of poetry or music (even though this would have been an especially appropriate scene for some melancholy director), they thought about uselessness and emptiness, but also about the strange sense of wholeness with which they are wrapped about. They thought: For what waters has our ship set sail? What rare bird sings deep within us? What is the path we are so confusedly flying towards through a dark universe?

In the bathetic context of the neat prosaic detail of the two friends not being able to get beyond the patrolled zone on the periphery of the volcano's crater and being dropped off there by unheroic taxi, this excessive passage both does and does not allow for taking the drama and the pathos seriously, does and does not believe in the textual construction of the power of death, is and is not lyrical. The sentimental surrender of the two friends and of the narrator to the temptation to fill the void with images and rhythms draws attention to a vital tension in Villena's writing: on the one hand 'it is true that behind the appetite for life lies death. And so whoever desperately loves to live is touched by a sudden beam of darkness. Perhaps at that moment the awareness of death – though not of dying – makes life itself impossible' (p.178); on the other hand

> ¿Quién no ha sentido la atracción del mundo? Pero la perfección – quizá – está en la inexistencia. Vivir es una turbación, una excrecencia inexplicable, y el puro, el pulquérrimo, quien no soporta lo agresivo de la imperfección, declara 'No hay que vivir, perfección es ausencia. O no, porque árboles, ríos, cuerpos que acarician . . .' (p.183)

> Who has not felt the pull of the world? But perfection – perhaps – lies in non-existence. To live is a disruption, an inexplicable excrescence,

and the pure, the immaculate, those who cannot bear the aggressions of imperfection declare: 'There is no need to live, perfection is absence. Or not, maybe, because the trees, rivers, bodies offering caresses . . .'

Caught between 'the pull of the world' and the impossible purity of absolute 'absence', Villena's writing engages in a constant disruption and yet affirmation of received cultural (and behavioural) values. Arturo's vertiginous attraction into the 'dark areas' in *Amour Passion* bring him to the grand illusion Love, but his narrating steers around it. *Boys* is replete with moments of abandonment and apotheosis but its redeemingly undefined characters collide, explode and move on, and spiritual union is with much tact touchingly avoided. Peter's dying fall into the darkness of Woman and Universe is revealed as an agreeable yet regrettable nonsense, not heroic, not redemptive and not the consummation of return. In some stories and poems theatricality, either as false-aware impassivity or obfuscating camp, at the very least postpones the closure which is the fulfilment of desire. In his discussion of feminist and gay autobiography in Spanish Smith finds that each of the texts he is writing about 'has moments in which the subject seeks to recognise him or herself in the phantasmal reflections of mirror, photograph, or printed text, moments in which a sense of self is at once reaffirmed and undermined' (*Laws*, p.19). When Villena constructs the mirrors, snapshots, film scenes, doorways, bedrooms and private stages which are his texts and gazes in (or is it out?) on his desires he both finds and constructs the flagrant and joyous presence of homoeroticism and adopts an explicitly dissident ethical stance. Yet – disruptively enough at the end of a half-century of theoretical, critical and creative movement away from such a position – what he is reaffirming as much as undermining here is a body of text which he insists is meant to stand for something very close to being a representation of a unique and particularly sensitive self. In these texts the narrating subject or the poet like to know life at least at one remove in order to know it better, but they also long to play a central role, not to be the absent other gazing on. There is an avid surrender to desire, but also an insistence on transgressing its terms, refusing its impositions of identity and position while also denying the temptation just simply to transcend it.

This attempt to live at the intersection of dissent and participation, to flee and to embrace the sensual and consuming world is embodied in the fantastical Madrid of so many of the texts. A place made up of fragments of history where the lines of different cultures and desires form a network of transgression, where eye-contact in a disco prompts both sexual desire and literary sparks of association:

> Y sí, ya sé que poco tiene que ver (o nada acaso),
> pero allí, entre la atmósfera de humo, y *rock,*
> y pésima ginebra me acordé del Lícidas
> de Horacio. Cuya belleza atrapa a los muchachos
> y ante el que caen rendidos y anhelantes las doncellas.
>
> (*Poesía*, pp.186–7)

> And yes, I know that it has little (or nothing even) to do with it / but there, in an atmosphere of smoke and heavy rock / and dreadful gin I remembered Lycidas / in Horace, whose beauty enthrals young men/ and before whom maidens fall stricken and desirous.[4]

This is a city, a New Spain, to be set against a contemporary cultural and political scene where, as Villena put it in 1989, 'we are invited to partake of the *new sobriety,* of *neoconservatism,* to join the *no coffee generation* (...) to see unorthodoxy as a bad thing, applaud the rigid family structure, discredit passion, abominate change, ideals and progress'.[5] In Villena's utopian space, enlivened by homoerotic encounters and discourses of difference, Western cultural history is compressed and subverted, made to take on a scandalous colouring. Rising shamelessly from the scene of bars and discos is 'un templo constuido alto, lleno de sol, / y abajo el mar azul, feliz, pleno de espuma . . .' (*Lugar*, pp.97–8: 'a temple built high up, full of sunlight,/ the blue sea below, joyful and replete with foam'). Here 'true unattainable happiness' can be embodied in the text, excessively and redemptively: 'Es un viento de magia y el olor de unas rosas. / [...] / El mágico tintín de una perfecta copa' (p.98: 'It is a breeze charged with magic and the smell of roses. / [...] / The enchanted chiming of a perfect wine-glass lightly struck'). The plodding culture of 'normal' modern life, not to mention the usual gravities and prejudices of literature, are countered with a camp hyper-awareness of the extremity of the situation and of the language deployed, with sex and seriousness, evasiveness and a perverse conviction:

4. The reference is to Horace, *Odes* I, iv.
5. Villena, 'La tentación del orden', *El País* (Madrid), 26 April 1989, p.13.

el denso, el menesteroso, el torpe,
el que sueña durezas y asperezas de vida,
pregunta sorpendido
¿quién es, de qué habláis, qué estáis diciendo?
¿por qué, tan de repente, os habéis puesto frívolos?

(Lugar, p.99)

then the dense, the busy, or the dull, / the one whose dreams are of the difficulties and the harshnesses of life / asks with surprise / Who is this? Who are you talking about? What are you saying? / Why have you all become so suddenly frivolous?

Blind to the directions of desire, possibly affronted by the object of its attentions and the excessiveness of its scenarios, this perplexed (male) onlooker is written out of the story, his values are resisted with deadly seriousness. For Villena, to write is to feel 'the pull of the world', his texts are a 'disruption', they refuse to compromise with ordinary experience and they dissent from conventional culture. Yet they lovingly engage with the specifics of experience, they become problematically enmeshed in sexual politics, they are as bonded to their cultural and counter-cultural heritage, to the processes of social change and personal involvement, as they are to the sensuality of language and action, to the necessity of rebellion and to the liberating irresponsibilities of creativity, individualism and desire.

Select Bibliography

Works by Villena (1970–1992)

Poetry

Poesía 1970–1984, Madrid, 1988
Comprising: *Sublime Solarium* (1971); *El viaje a Bizancio* (1978: *The Journey to Byzantium*); *Hymnica* (1979); *Huir del invierno* (1981: *To Flee From Winter*); *La muerte únicamente* (1984: *Death Alone*)
Marginados, Valencia, 1986 (*Poems on the Margins*)
Como a lugar extraño, Madrid, 1990 (*As To A Foreign Place*)

Prose Narrative

Ante el espejo: memorias de una adolescencia, Barcelona, 1982 (*In Front of the Mirror: Memoirs of an Adolescence*)
Amor pasión, Barcelona, 1986 (*Amour Passion*) (first edition, without the concluding 'Carta final', 1983)
Chicos, Madrid, 1989 (*Boys*)
Fuera del mundo, Barcelona, 1992 (*Beyond the World*)

Essays, Biographical Studies and Introductions

Corsarios de guante amarillo, Barcelona, 1983 (*Corsairs in Yellow Gloves*)
La tentación de Ícaro, Barcelona, 1986 (*The Temptation of Icarus*)
Yo, Miguel Ángel Buonarroti, Barcelona, 1990 (*I, Michelangelo Buonarroti*)
'Vicente Aleixandre, el surrealismo y *Pasión de la tierra*', in Vicente Aleixandre, *Pasión de la tierra*, ed. Villena, Madrid, 1976, pp.11–92
'Lapitas y centauros: (Algunas consideraciones sobre la nueva poesía española en la última década)', *Quimera* (Barcelona), no. 12 (October 1981), pp.13–20
'La contracultura', in Fernando Savater and Luis Antonio de Villena

(jt. authors), *Heterodoxias y contracultura*, Barcelona, 1982, pp.87–157

'La sensibilidad homoerótica en el *Romancero gitano*', *Campus* (Granada), no. 27 (December 1986), pp.27–31

'La tentación del orden', *El País* (Madrid), 26 April 1989, p.13

Critical and Theoretical Works by Others

Alas, Leopoldo, 'Notas para una lectura heterodoxa de la obra poética de Luis Antonio de Villena,' *Cuadernos Hispanoamericanos* (Madrid), no. 475 (1990), pp.146–8

de Lauretis, Teresa, 'The Violence of Rhetoric: Considerations on representation and gender', in Teresa de Lauretis (ed.), *Technologies of Gender*, Bloomington, Indiana, 1987

Dollimore, Jonathan, *Sexual Dissidence. Augustine to Wilde, Freud to Foucault*, Oxford, 1991

Dyer, Richard, *Now You See It: Studies on Lesbian and Gay Film*, London, 1990

Jiménez, José Olivio, 'La poesía de Luis Antonio de Villena', in Luis Antonio de Villena, *Poesía 1970–1984*, Madrid, 1988, pp.9–64

Litoral (Málaga), no. 188 (November 1990). Special issue: *Luis Antonio de Villena. Sobre un pujante deseo*

Sahuquillo, Angel, *Federico García Lorca y la cultura de la homosexualidad masculina*, Alicante, 1991

Sedgwick, Eve Kosofsky, *Epistemology of the Closet*, New York, 1990

Smith, Paul Julian, *Laws of Desire: Questions of Homosexuality in Spanish Writing and Film 1960–1990*, Oxford, 1992

Woods, Gregory, *Articulate Flesh: Male homoeroticism and modern poetry*, Yale, 1987

Further bibliographical information is to be found in:

García Rodríguez, Javier, 'De la belleza al deseo. Del deseo a la muerte: aproximación a la obra poética de Luis Antonio de Villena', *Tropelías* (Zaragoza), no. 2 (1991), pp.41–7: pp.46–7

Perriam, Chris, 'Reality and the Angels: Luis Antonio de Villena and *La muerte únicamente*', *Bulletin of Hispanic Studies* (Liverpool), no. 67 (1990), pp.31–42: p.40

Index